Jessie and Ridley

They Made a Difference

Ridley Wills II

☙❧

BY: RIDLEY WILLS II

Aknowledgements

In early March 2008, I broke my hip when I fell while chasing a ball thrown by my four-year-old grandson, Morgan J. Wills, Jr. Frustrated by my inability to drive an automobile in the weeks immediately following surgery to put pins and a plate in my hip, I was fortunate to be able to focus much attention to my manuscript. As soon as I could get in and out of my car, I drove down to Shelbyville, Tennessee, where my Ely and Whiteside ancestors lived and spent some time in Willow Mount Cemetery inspecting tombstones on the Whiteside lot. The two men I spoke to at the cemetery office were very helpful and courteous then and later. Last winter, before my fall, I drove to Brownsville, Tennessee, where my grandfather, Ridley Wills, grew up. I stayed overnight with my fourth cousin, Pat H. Mann, Jr. and his wife, Ann. I appreciate their friendship and gracious hospitality, that included a barbeque lunch Ann prepared the day I arrived. Before then, Pat, an attorney, had already searched legal records in the Haywood County Courthouse and made copies of various deeds and wills involving the Wills family. Earlier, I had learned from Pat the circumstances of the death of my great uncle, Mann Wills, in 1936. While I was at the Haywood County Library, Pat called to suggest that I accompany him to a nearby warehouse where he showed me the bronze plaque dedicating the Haywood Memorial Hospital to the memory of Dr. and Mrs. William Thadeus Wills in 1930. Pat is working to have the plaque installed at the museum on College Hill in Brownsville. He has been a great help on family matters relating to Haywood County for a number of years

Once I had a complete manuscript for my book, *Jessie and Ridley: They Made a Difference*, I sent copies to my sister, Ellen Wills Martin, in Washington, D.C., and to my brother, Matt B. Wills, in Colorado Springs. They both remembered stories and facts I either did not know or had forgotten. I am grateful to them for their help that, in Ellen's case, included lending me family photographs. My first cousin, Phoebe Clark Nischan, also lent me family photographs that enhance the book. Phoebe's sister, Eleanor Clark Kelley, was good enough to read the manuscript and reassure me that the book would be well-received. Phoebe and Eleanor's brother, George Wills Crook, was helpful with his memories of Far Hills, our grandmother's home. Eleanor's daughters, Craig Kelley Adkisson and Josephine Kelley Darwin, both remember their great grandmother, Mamma Wills. They shared funny stories of her and of their grandmother, Mamie Craig Crook, and her husband Senter C. Crook. I appreciate their help.

Mann Wills Ogleby is a long-time friend and second cousin. He well remembers his grandparents, Mann and Della Wills, and gave me interesting information about them and their lives that I would not have been able to find elsewhere. We enjoyed delving together in our Wills ancestry.

Late in the process, I was able to contact two second cousins on the Ely side of my family, W. Frederick Williams III, and his sister, Margaret Williams Smith, contemporaries of mine and grandchildren of my grandmother's half sister, Charlotte Ely Nelson. Because Fred and Margaret live in Maynard, Massachusetts and Guilford, Connecticut, respectively, we had not kept in touch in recent years, How much fun it was to reconnect and add to my story information on their grandmother and her family. E-mails make getting information so much easier and faster.

One of my prized possessions was a photograph of my great grandfather, William Thadeus Wills, M.D. My father's first cousin, Elizabeth Wills, gave it to me when she moved, late in life, to Nashville. My son, Morgan J. Wills, now has the picture as he too is a physician. Elizabeth and I both kept in touch with her nephew, John Thadeus Wills, of Versailles, Kentucky, whose father, William Ridley Wills II, was a Fugitive poet with my father, Jesse Wills in the 1920s. Ridley II was named for his uncle, Ridley Wills, for whom I was also named. Because we were given identical names, occasionally acquaintances, particularly ones from West Tennessee, would get us confused. For two decades before his death in 2006, Ridley II's son, John Thaddeus Wills, and I were good friends. I am sorry that Thad did not live to see this book published. Fortunately, I have established a relationship with his son, Matt Wills, of Lexington, Kentucky, and am grateful to him for lending me a valuable photograph of our common ancestor, Asa Mann (1799-1870).

One of my grandmother Wills' favorite people was Trousdale

Wills Sturdivant, another first cousin of my father's. Trousdale was a wonderful comfort to my grandmother late in her life. Trousdale's daughter, Virginia Sturdivant Dobson, and Virginia's daughter, Marie Dodson Maxwell, are other extended family members who have helped me in my research. Marie is Dean of Students at Harpeth Hall School in Nashville, where my granddaughter, Meade Wills, is a freshman. They both take pleasure in knowing they are kin even if they don't know exactly how. Maybe they will when they read my book.

For nearly thirty years, Ridley Wills' closest business associate was C. A. "Neely" Craig. Mr. Craig's granddaughter, Margaret Ann Craig Robinson, and I cherish the fact that our respective families have been good friends for four generations. Margaret Ann was kind enough to read my manuscript and write a forward to it on the cover.

I am grateful to Lynne Hutchinson, at Vanderbilt, who has now edited two of my books and to Caroline Sanney, graphic designer, who designed this one. Finally, through my friendship with John P. Campbell, Lightning Source, Inc., of LaVergne, Tennessee, printed this book. Without the competent attention of Lynne, Caroline and Lightning Source, Inc., the manuscript would still be in a three-ring binder on my office shelf.

Cover Photos:
Jessie Ely Wills and William Ridley Wills

Published by Ridley Wills II
Edited by Lynne Hutchison
Designed by Caroline Sanney
Printed and distributed by Lightning Source, Inc., La Vergne, Tennessee

Chapters

CHAPTER I

The middle of September 1871 was pretty normal in Brownsville, Tennessee. The activity would pick up in a week or two when farmers would begin driving their wagons, loaded with cotton, across rutted roads to the numerous gins scattered across Haywood County. The gin in the Ninth District, where the Bond, Estes, and Wills families had farms, was just north of Cypress Creek, on or close to J.R. Bond's place.

In a few days, Dr. William Thaddeus Wills would celebrate his 43rd birthday at his home on a lot bounded on the north by Short Street, on the south by Burton Street, on the west by Factory Street and on the east by Kinney and Freeman Streets.[1] His wife, the former Elizabeth Winona "Lizzie" Mann, who was only 23, planned the event with the help of her black servant, Aunt Martha, and her widowed mother, Martha Epps Mann, then 57. It would be simple because Lizzie was in her ninth month of pregnancy. It seems likely that Mrs. Mann's sister, Eva Mann Moore, and Eva's husband, Billy Moore, would stop by to offer their congratulations and to see Lizzie and William's little boy, Asa Mann Wills, then 16 months old.

Lizzie and Dr. Wills, who had been her family physician since she was a little girl, had married on June 22, 1869, when she was 21 and he nearly 41. Old enough to be her father, Wills was still in the prime of life. Standing six feet tall and weighing 180 pounds, he had, a friend remembered, "sandy hair, blue eyes, a full but short reddish-brown beard, and no surplus flesh." His fellow physicians respected his medical opinions, recognized his ability and knew him to be ethical and respectable. Many of his patients idolized him. Townspeople also considered Dr. Wills to be one of the luckiest men in the community, as Lizzie was "well born, well reared, a toast, a wit and wealthy."[2]

---

1   The C.C. Beers 1978 Map of Haywood County, Tenn., shows W.T. Wills' name at this location. Mrs. William Thaddeus Wills owned the property at her death on Oct. 21, 1907. Factory Street was later renamed McLemore Street.

2   Response made by Dr. John Sevier at the dedication of the Haywood County Memorial Hospital, The Brownsville States-Gazette, Jan. 4, 1931.

Three months before they married, Dr. Wills purchased from Edward Claiborne Sturdivant, Sr., a one-acre lot on the south side of Key Corner Road for $850.[3] He subdivided the lot and sold the pieces a few years later. In March 1870, Lizzie's dad, Asa Mann, a wealthy farmer, gave her a four-acre lot adjoining the Meale Academy and Johnson Road. That happened only three months before Mr. Mann died at age 70.

Asa Mann (1799–1870)

Lizzie and William's second baby, born September 19, 1871, turned out to be another boy. He was named William after his father. To distinguish between the two, the baby would always be known by his middle name "Ridley." The Wills, like so many Southerners, often used family names as Christian names. They had already named their first son Asa Mann Wills, born May 1, 1870, for Lizzie's father, and thought Ridley would be just as fitting a name for their second son. Ridley was Dr. Wills' mother's maiden name. Dr. Wills was proud of her for having the strength and fortitude to bring him and his siblings to Haywood County from Virginia in 1840 after her husband, William Wills, died. As children, William Thaddeus and his three

William Thaddeus Wills, M.D.
(1828–1878)

unmarried sisters had lived on the farm Mrs. Wills had bought west of town in a section of the 9th District known as "Moore's town."

Brownsville, where Ridley Wills grew up and for which he held a lifelong affection, was on the L&N Railroad 56 miles east of Memphis. At the close of the war, six years before he was born, Brownsville had

---

3   E.C. Sturdivant, Jr. was president of Sturdivant's Old Virginia Style Brunswick Stew, packed by Sturdivant Packing Co. in Brownsville, Tenn., and distributed across the South.

about 1,200 inhabitants but had grown somewhat since then. In 1874, there were about 21,000 people in the county, 9,400 white and 11,600 colored. Although most of the town's first settlers came from North Carolina, the Manns and Wills came from Amelia County, Va., just west of Richmond, where decades of tobacco cultivation had depleted the soil. Two traits that the descendants of these early settlers shared were those of conservatism and of pride in their Virginia heritage.

The Hatchie River, navigable by shallow-draft steamboats, drained the southern part of the county, while the slightly smaller Forked Deer River drained the northern half. In the 1850s, before the railroad came to Brownsville, citizens there depended on steamboats to bring their groceries from Memphis on the Hatchie, which was closer to town than the Forked Deer. The dividing line separating what was known as "Forked Deer Country" from "Hatchie Country" was a ridge on the very backbone of which stood the Haywood County Courthouse.
Cypress grew along the many fine creek and river bottoms, and there was an abundance of hardwood timber all over the county, with gum, poplar, several varieties of oak and other hardwoods. Cotton was the staple crop; the average yield of cotton in 1874 was 250 pounds of lint cotton per acre. Once ginned, the bales were taken on the L&N Railroad to Memphis, the principal cotton market for the Midsouth.

In town there were five doctors, including Dr. Wills, and seven lawyers, including two Bonds, one Estes, one Folk and one Mann. Dr. Wills had moved from his 600-acre farm to Brownsville because it had enough white families to warrant a school. After Mrs. John Bertie Moore and Dr. Wills moved to town, there were only three white families living in the ninth district. One was J.J. Moore, bachelor son of Mr. and Mrs. John B. Moore. White farmers in Haywood County often sent their boys to boarding schools, such as to William R. "Sawney" Webb's school in Culleoka, Tennessee, that opened in 1870. The first public school in Haywood County was the Brownsville Grammar School, which opened in the mid-1970s. Mann, Ridley and their little sister, Virginia "Jennie," who was born in 1876, either attended it or private schools, of which there were several.

Dr. Wills, who honed his skills as a surgeon while serving in the Confederate Army, had an extensive medical practice across the county.

He made his rounds by horseback or in a buggy pulled over roads that were bad all year long and frequently impassable in January and February. Because there was no hospital closer than Jackson, he delivered babies, black and white, in their parents' homes and performed appendectomies and other surgical procedures in the same places, often using a dining room table or a portable table he brought. In 1874, when his boys were four and three, Dr. Wills bought two mules and a two-horse wagon for his farm. Two years later, he and A.E. Sangster formed a partnership to operate a drugstore on the corner of the public square and Washington Street. His motive was probably to save money on drugs, as well as to supplement his meager income as a physician and farmer in a county that still had not recovered from the Civil War. Dr. Wills was the only physician in town who owned his own office, a one-story frame building on College Street.[4]

Life was precarious in Haywood County in the 1870s as, annually, yellow fever and other contagious diseases swept through the county taking the lives of many, particularly children. Early in her womanhood, Lizzie Wills contracted measles, and for the remainder of her life she was physically frail. In 1873, after an unusually severe winter, there was an epidemic of contagious diseases and a financial panic. Poor sanitation made the situation worse.

Dr. Wills treated patients for cholera, malaria, smallpox and yellow fever that summer. Even he, with a medical degree from the nation's most prestigious medical school, Jefferson Medical College in Philadelphia, could not save his infant daughter, Martha Epps, "Eppie," their third child. She died at home on Oct. 10, 1873. The sadness of her death was assuaged somewhat by the birth of Lizzie and William's fourth child, Martha Cousins, on Dec. 29, 1873. But Martha lived only nine months and was buried next to Eppie in Brownsville's Oakwood Cemetery in October 1874.

That was the year of one of the worst droughts in Haywood County history, lasting from April 18 to October 6. The next summer, there was so little corn that farmers literally counted each grain. In 1875, malaria attacked a member of practically every family in town.

---

4   In 1932, the Hotchkiss-Lyle store stood on the site of Dr. Wills' office.

The Wills' youngest child, Virginia, nicknamed "Jennie," was born October 7. 1876. She was the only sister that Mann and Ridley would remember as she lived to see her twenty-first birthday before dying of typhoid fever on January 4, 1898. In 1933, a friend gave Mann a picture of Jennie that he cherished and quickly shared with Ridley. Before she died, Jennie lived with Mann and his wife, Della.

The loss of two precious baby girls in 1873 and 1874 may have intensified the tender feelings that Lizzie Wills always harbored for the less fortunate in the community. At the dedication of the Haywood County Hospital on Dec. 31, 1930, Dr. John H. Sevier paid tribute to Lizzie. He said, "She was always seeking some unfortunate one to do some kind, charitable act for, and she never allowed her left hand to know what her right hand was doing. No one knew her but to love her; to associate with her was a benediction!"

The Wills probably were Methodists, the faith of Lizzie's family. In numbers and wealth, this denomination ranked second in Brownsville, with Baptists ranking first and Presbyterians third. The other denominations were numerically and financially weak.

There were two weekly newspapers in town, the *Brownsville Bee* and the *Brownsville States*, both of which were Democratic. Dr. and Mrs. Wills read both, as well as the Memphis *Avalanche*. Mrs. Wills usually shopped for her family on the public square and on Depot Street, making sure that she was home in time to have dinner and supper with her husband and children. She was fortunate to have "Aunt Martha," her faithful black mammy, prepare the meals. At Hiram Mann and Sons, on the south side of the public square, Mrs. Wills could find dry goods and staples. On rare occasions, Dr. Wills would shop there for gents' furnishings. Across the public square, C.A. Ogden sold stoves and tin ware, wood and willowware, and house furnishings. All the merchants knew and appreciated Lizzie Wills, whom they called "Miss Lizzie." Sometimes, she would stop in the Brownsville Savings Bank and chat with Mr. R. S. Thomas, the president, who always was delighted to see her.

CHAPTER II

WHO WERE HIS PEOPLE?

As bad as the early and mid-1870s were, nothing prepared Lizzie for the unexpected loss of her husband on September 26, 1878, two weeks after he celebrated his 50th birthday. His death came in the great yellow fever epidemic that paralyzed so many Mississippi Valley towns and cities, including Memphis and Brownsville. On the day he died, Dr. Wills was out in the country, making house calls on yellow fever victims. When he didn't come home, Lizzie became concerned. The worst possible news arrived; someone told her that her husband had been found dead, propped up against a tree, his horse still standing nearby. Yellow fever didn't kill Dr. Wills, a heart attack did. His unexpected death left Lizzie with three children, ranging in age from two to eight, and, for the first time in her life, real responsibility. With the loss of his love, his wise counsel and his medical practice income, she had an enormous burden, being called on to be both mother and father to Mann, Ridley and Jennie. Lizzie bore her burden bravely, as did so many Southern women of her generation. Owing to her frail constitution, she had difficulty in disciplining the boys, particularly Mann, whom Aunt Martha described as "a cantankerous roarer." When Mann wouldn't mind, Mrs. Wills called in Aunt Martha, who "brung him up with a hickory," and "brung him up frequently." Despite having to discipline Mann a great deal, Aunt Martha showered the three Wills children with love and devotion. Martha's husband, Uncle Alfred, who also worked for the Wills, also was a positive influence on the children. Mann and Ridley would never forget the folklore he shared with them when they were little boys.

Mrs. Wills was a very good seamstress who used her sewing machine to make clothes for her children. However, she was not strong enough to push the pedal. Little Ridley, who had a sweet disposition, would sit on the floor and push the pedal with his hands.

One example of Mann's mischievousness came when he was a little older. One autumn day, he climbed an apple tree hanging over the street. When an elderly gentleman walked under the tree, Mann dropped an apple that landed squarely on top of the man's stovepipe hat. He looked up, spotted Mann, and said, "Mann, Ridley wouldn't have done that." Neighbors and Lizzie's family members, such as Aunt Eva Moore, also were generous in helping her properly rear her children. One friend, a Mr. Wilson, often took Mann and Ridley to the Presbyterian Church and then to Sunday dinner at his home. In September 1888, when Mann was 18 years old, he was admitted to full membership in First Presbyterian Church "on examination of his religious experiences."[5]

Despite living on a very tight budget, Mrs. Wills was anxious that her children not feel deprived. One Christmas, she gave Ridley a Barlow knife that he especially treasured. The children never felt less privileged than their friends.

As Dr. Wills died before his children were old enough to comprehend and retain stories of his heritage, Lizzie filled them in as best she could from what her husband had told her. She definitely knew that she and Dr. Wills were cousins, although in different generations. Her great grandfather, Thomas Tabb Wills, was a brother of Dr. Wills' father, William Wills. Lizzie undoubtedly told them that most of their ancestors came from England to the Colony of Virginia in the 17th century, and that their father had been born in Jetersburg, Dinwiddie County, Virginia, near Petersburg, on September 11, 1829.

Emanuel Wills (emigrant from Bristol, England)
Elizabeth Cary *b* 1653 (Bristol, England)
m <1670

|

Capt. Miles Wills, *d* 1734
Hannah Scarbrook, *d* >1702
m 1690–1685

|

Matthew Wills (*c* 1696–1760)
Mary Armstead, *d* 1766

|

---

5   First Presbyterian Church Session minutes, September 29, 1888. Mann's children, Ridley, Trousdale and Harriette joined First Presbyterian on September 6, 1908; August 22, 1909; and July 3, 1910, respectively.

Col. Lawrence Wills (1732–1784)
Anne Pryor (*c* 1730–1801)

|

William Wills (<1785–< 1840)
Ridley Branch, *b* 1790
m 1811

|

William Thaddeus Wills (1828–1878)
Elizabeth Winona "Lizzie" Mann (1848–1907)
m 1869

Asa Mann Wills (1870–1936) Della Womack (1874–1953) *m* 1893	Wm. Ridley Wills (1871–1949) Jessie Ely (1872–1965) *m* 1898	Virginia Wills (1876-1898)

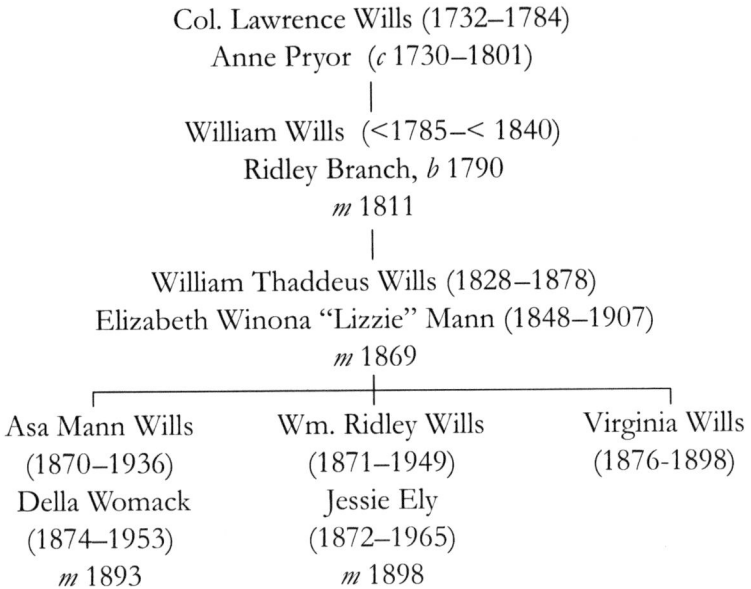

The first Wills to come to America was Emanuel Wills, who emigrated from Bristol, England, in the latter half of the 1600s. His wife was Elizabeth Cary, a native of Bristol, England, whom Emanuel married in Virginia before 1670. Elizabeth was one of seven children of Col. Miles Cary, who immigrated to Warwick County, Colony of Virginia, about 1645. There he gained wealth and prominence, acquiring several thousand acres, numerous slaves, a mill, a store and membership in the Virginia House of Burgesses from 1660 to 1665. He was an officer in the Virginia militia from 1654 until his death in 1667. Colonel Cary was commander of the English forces at Old Point Comfort, Virginia, when the Dutch attacked on June 10, 1667. Mortally wounded, Col. Cary died five days later. He was Dr. William Thaddeus Wills' fourth great grandfather and his wife, Lizzie's sixth great grandfather.

Dr. Wills' mother, Ridley Branch Wills, was named for her grandmother, Ridley Jones, the first person in the family known to have that first name. The Branches had been in Virginia even longer than the Wills, having emigrated earlier in the 1600s, living first in Henrico County and later in Chesterfield and Amelia counties. Christopher Branch probably was the first member of the Branch family to come to Virginia. Ridley Jones married Matthew Branch, Christopher's great, great grandson, in 1749 in Amelia County, VA. Their son, Peter Branch, also married in Amelia County in 1785. His wife was the former Judith Jones. They were Ridley Branch Wills' parents.

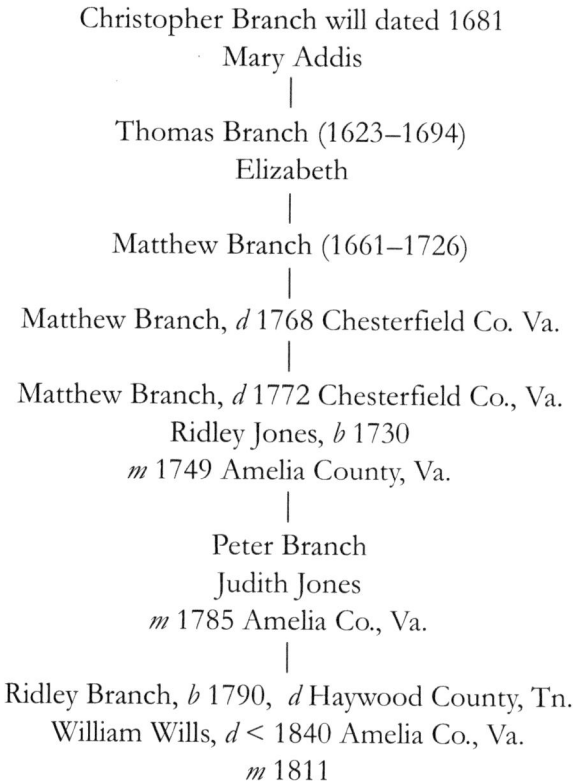

Christopher Branch will dated 1681
Mary Addis
|
Thomas Branch (1623–1694)
Elizabeth
|
Matthew Branch (1661–1726)
|
Matthew Branch, *d* 1768 Chesterfield Co. Va.
|
Matthew Branch, *d* 1772 Chesterfield Co., Va.
Ridley Jones, *b* 1730
m 1749 Amelia County, Va.
|
Peter Branch
Judith Jones
m 1785 Amelia Co., Va.
|
Ridley Branch, *b* 1790, *d* Haywood County, Tn.
William Wills, *d* < 1840 Amelia Co., Va.
m 1811

Lizzie's children knew that their father had six sisters, Carrie, Amanda, Lucy, Martha, Addie and Virginia; and three brothers, Richard, Willis and Peter Branch Wills. They also heard stories of how, soon after their grandfather died, their grandmother, Ridley Branch Wills, and four unmarried children, including their then 12-year-old dad, came by wagon from Virginia to Haywood County. In Haywood County, he went to one of the local subscription schools or academies. That he was able to later attend and graduate from Jefferson Medical College suggests that his father had some financial means.

After graduating from Jefferson Medical College, Dr. Wills returned to Haywood County to practice medicine. He did so until the Civil War broke out in 1861. On September 20 of that year, Dr. Wills was appointed a Second Lieutenant of Company D, 31st Infantry Regiment, Confederate States Army. The regiment had been organized at Trenton, Tennessee, that summer. At that time, A.H. Bradford of Brownsville was elected its colonel; Dr. Wills' friendship with Mr. Bradford probably influenced him to join the regiment. The 31st Regiment was at Columbus, Kentucky, in December 1861 and January 1862. When Fort Donelson fell in February 1862, the regiment fell back to Tiptonville and then Fort Pillow. Ordered to Corinth, Mississippi, to aid in checking the advance of the Federal Army after the Battle of Shiloh in April 1862, the regiment marched to Tupelo and then rode the cars, via Mobile, to Chattanooga. The regiment took part in General Bragg's invasion of Kentucky in the summer of 1862.

On September 25, 1862, during the Kentucky campaign, Lt. Wills was appointed assistant surgeon of the 31st Regiment. His new rank was retroactive to July 21, 1862. Dr. Wills must have been extremely busy amputating limbs of the Confederate soldiers wounded in the Battle of Perryville that took place October 8, 1862. After retreating through Cumberland Gap to Knoxville, the regiment moved to Murfreesboro where it was heavily engaged in the Battle of Stones River as part of Cheatham's Division. On January 4, 1863, the regiment was ordered to Shelbyville and then to Chattanooga where it arrived on August 25, 1863. The regiment fought in the Battle of Chickamauga on September 19, 1863, and remained in the Chattanooga area before falling back to Dalton, Georgia, after the Battle of Missionary Ridge.

On October 10, 1863, Dr. Wills tendered his resignation from the Confederate Army. His resignation was accepted by Jefferson Davis, President of the Confederate States of America, to take effect October 22, 1863.[6] Dr. Wills, then 35 years old, returned to Haywood County with an honorable discharge to resume his medical practice and, four years after the war ended, marry Lizzie Mann.

---

6   Letter, The Adjutant General, War Department, to Honorable Kenneth McKellar, United States Senate, September 18, 1931, Copy in the collection of the author.

Lizzie knew considerably more about her own family. She grew up on her family farm a few miles north of town. Her father, Asa Mann, was a cotton farmer and a moneylender. He had come to Haywood County from Amelia County, Virginia, in 1836 when he was 37, with his wife, Martha Epps Cousins Mann, Lizzie's mother. They had married February 25, 1833, in Amelia County. Lizzie's grandfather, Joel Mann, married Elizabeth "Eliza" Cousins Wills, the widow of Matthew Wills, in 1798, six years after his first wife, Francis Wilson Mann, died. Joel and Eliza had six children.

The first Mann to move to Haywood County was Joel's son by his first wife. William A. Wilson Mann, who came no later than 1828, built the first grist mill in Haywood County. Impressed with the fertility of the land, he convinced his father to come. In 1830, Joel had 48 slaves and extensive holdings in three Virginia counties. Unfortunately, most of his land was worn out. Consequently, in 1831 he sold his land in Virginia, followed his son's advice and moved with Eliza and another son, Austin, to Haywood County. The move took several weeks and was done overland with many wagons carrying their possessions and servants. Other sons and daughters, all of whom had married, followed their father and brothers to Haywood County over the next few years. Three, Elizabeth Mann Scott, Frances Mann Rudd and Richard Mann, chose to stay in Virginia with their young families. A decade later, in Haywood County, when Joel was 67 years old, he had given most of his slaves to his children. Nevertheless, he still owned 19 slaves, 12 male and 7 female, good land, and had interests in a cotton gin and a grist mill. He was, at his death on November 15, 1844, a wealthy man. When Eliza Mann wrote her last will and testament nine years later, she gave her four granddaughters between $700 and $1,000 each, and gave $700 each to her sons, Wily and Asa Mann, and her step-daughter Martha Ann. Because Eliza and Joel Mann's other son, Austin Mann, had inherited his father's farm and received a monetary bequest at his death, she left him only a nominal amount.

Robert Mann, *d* 1713
Isabel

|

Francis Mann, *d* 1753
Elizabeth

|

Cain Mann, *d* 1807
Mary

|

Joel Mann (1773–1844)
Elizabeth Cousins Wills
m 1798

|

Asa Mann (1799–1870)
Martha Epps Cousins
m 1833

|

Elizabeth Winona "Lizzie" Mann (1848–1907)
William Thaddeus Wills (1828–1878)
m 1869

Eliza Wills' son, Mann, attended whatever grammar and secondary schools Brownsville afforded. In 1892, he graduated from Cumberland Law School in Lebanon, Tennessee. Mann must have worked his way through law school as his mother could not have afforded the tuition. After graduation, he returned to Brownsville to practice law.

Because of his mother's precarious financial condition, Ridley quit school after the eighth grade and went to work in Brownsville to help support his family. Virginia also probably quit school after the eighth grade. Ridley first worked in a store in Brownsville but wanted to experience a broader world in some field of work where he could excel. He was both ambitious and bright, and despite his limited education, was good with figures.

In 1884, a Brownsville girl Mattie Walker married Robert S. Fletcher of Jackson, Tennessee. Mrs. Wills and Ridley knew Mattie, who died in 1886, and heard from time to time how successful Mr. Fletcher had become in Jackson. Mrs. Wills knew he was a partner in Burkett & Fletcher, a growing wholesale and retail grocery business, an ardent worker for the Democratic Party and a respected citizen.

Dissatisfied with his work in Brownsville, Ridley asked Mr. Fletcher for a position as clerk in his store in Jackson. At the interview, Ridley was forthright. He told Mr. Fletcher that he knew nothing about the grocery business, but that he could learn. At the end of the interview, Mr. Fletcher gave Ridley a job and assured him that he was not concerned in the least about Ridley's lack of experience. Mr. Fletcher could see that the young man had a quick mind, an "ambition to learn" and possessed character and integrity. He invited Ridley to spend the night in his home, as Brownsville was 28 long miles away. Before retiring that night, Mr. Fletcher gave Ridley some books on bookkeeping. The next morning, Mr. Fletcher's second wife, Pattie Walker Fletcher, discovered that Ridley's bed had not been slept in. She mentioned this to her husband, who asked Ridley about it. Ridley said that he had stayed up all night studying the Burkett & Fletcher books. Years later, Mr. Fletcher said that

Ridley was the best clerk who ever worked for him and that, when the young man had an opportunity to accept a job in the State Treasurer's Office in Nashville, he "gave him up" knowing that Ridley would, one day, attain heights as "a wonderful man and business leader."[7]

In 1893, when he was only 22 years old, Mann was elected to the Tennessee State Legislature. In Nashville, Mann met and fell in love with Della Womack, a 17- or 18-year-old girl from Warren County, who had come to Nashville to work as an engrossing clerk. She was boarding with Reverend and Mrs. Marcus B. DeWitt at their home at 711 Woodland St. The Womacks had known the DeWitts when Rev. DeWitt was minister of the Cumberland Presbyterian Church in McMinnville. Della had grown up knowing the DeWitts' son, John, who was in law school in 1893. One of Della's other suitors was Cordell Hull.[8] Della and Mann married in 1893 at the little church near Dibrell, Tennessee, where the Womacks were members. The reception was at the nearby Womack farm despite inclement weather. The storm intensified so much during the reception that evening that the bride and groom and some of the wedding guests were forced to spend the night at the farm. Because the house was crowded, one of Della's little sisters had to sleep at the foot of the bride and groom's bed.

Della's father, George Washington Womack, was a mule trader and horse trader in McMinnville, in addition to being a farmer. After Della and Mann married, he moved to Mississippi where the explosion in cotton growing around the turn of the century made mule trading a very lucrative business.

Della and Mann's first child, Della Trousdale Wills was born in 1894. As the state legislature met for the first three months of every other year, Mann lived in a rooming house in Nashville for the first three months of the year in 1895 and 1897, and was back in Brownville with Della and Trousdale for the balance of those years.

---

7   Remarks of Col. Robert S. Fletcher made August 29, 1924 at National Life and Accident Insurance Company picnic at Jackson, Tennessee.

8   Cordell Hull was elected to the U.S. Senate in 1930. President Roosevelt named him Secretary of State in 1933. He held that position until November 1944, when he resigned for failing health. In 1945, Hull was awarded the Nobel Peace Prize for his efforts to establish world peace and for his work in establishing the United Nations.

In 1893, Edward Burr Craig, cashier of the People's National Bank in Pulaski, resigned to become State Treasurer. In Nashville, he met Mann Wills, a new legislator. As treasurer, the 34-year-old Craig also was Tennessee Insurance Commissioner. Possibly, Mann introduced E.B. to his brother Ridley. Another possibility is that Reau E. Folk, a young man from Brownsville, who was Chief Clerk of the House of Representatives, made the introduction. Regardless of how they met, Craig offered Ridley a job in the Treasurer's office. Ridley accepted, resigned his job in Jackson and moved to Nashville as a clerk in Mr. Craig's office at the state capitol. There, in 1897, he would meet E.B. Craig's brother, C.A. "Neely" Craig, who joined the insurance department after disposing of his interest in a drugstore in Pulaski.

In 1895 and again in 1897, Mann Wills was Clerk of the Senate. With an outgoing personality, he got to know aspiring politicians from all over the state. One was T. Leigh Thompson, a state legislator from Lewisburg, whose roommate while he was in the Senate was Cordell Hull. At the time, Thompson was dating Miss Eleanor "Nellie" Ely, Maid of Honor for Tennessee at the Confederate Reunion at Richmond in 1896, and vice-president of the Nashville Chapter of the Daughters of the Confederacy. Nellie, who was 25 at the time of the reunion, was one of the belles of the state, being described in the *Nashville American* as "Young, beautiful and irresistible. Her beaming gray eyes look through sweeping lashes and under exquisitely-arched brows." Governor Robert Taylor was so taken with Nellie that he appointed her a lieutenant colonel on his staff and presented her with a jeweled sword and belt that she wore as an official representative for Tennessee at the Tennessee Centennial Celebration in 1897. Nellie seemed to have inherited her beauty. Miss Maggie Whiteside, her aunt, was counted the Belle of the South during the Civil War and "was noted everywhere for her transcendent beauty and exquisite loveliness." Still another aunt, Miss Ada Whiteside, "startled all Europe with her beauty, and, later as Mrs. James Mather, was counted the handsomest woman in New York during her residence there prior to her untimely death" a few years before the Confederate reunion at Richmond.[9]

---

9   Americus, Ga. *Times-Recorder*, 1896

Nellie, who was born November 11, 1870, had three sisters: Mary "Mamie" born in 1867; Jessie, born September 11, 1872, and Ruth, born April 5, 1873. Mamie, Nellie and Jessie also had a half-sister, Charlotte, born in 1876, and a half-brother, William Edward, born in 1878. Their father, Jesse Ely, was a Nashville businessman. Ruth Chaffin Whiteside Ely, the mother of Mamie, Nellie, Jessie and Ruth, died April 8, 1873, three days after Ruth was born. Mrs. Ely, only 30 years old at the time of her death, was buried in her father's lot at Willow Mount Cemetery in her hometown of Shelbyville. Baby Ruth lived only seven months, dying November 21, 1873. Without a wife, Jesse needed help to rear his three remaining daughters. He couldn't turn to his mother, Charlotte Jamison Ely, as she was not in good health and was soon to die. Ruth's mother, Margaret Ann Whiteside, lived in Shelbyville, and wasn't available. The only mother Jessie would remember was her stepmother and aunt, Mary Whiteside Mitchell Ely, who married Jesse Ely not long after her sister, Ruth, died. In 1880, Mr. and Mrs. Ely, Mamie, Nellie, Jessie, Charlotte, Edward, and Mrs. Ely's sixteen-year-old daughter, Maggie, by her first husband, Captain Thomas R. Mitchell, lived at 321 N. Vine Street, one of Nashville's premier residential streets. A black servant, 25-year-old Addie Williams, also lived there, possibly in a carriage house to the rear.

In 1896, Ridley Wills was promoted to deputy insurance commissioner. He also was invited, about this time, by Mr. Ely to board in his home. Ridley was delighted to accept as the Elys lived in a fine house only a block away from his job at the State Capitol. More importantly, he was dating another of Mr. Ely's beautiful daughters, Jessie. As a young girl, the outgoing Jessie had the ambition to become a bareback rider for a circus. By the time she graduated from the gentile Ward's Seminary, Jessie probably had dropped that idea. Just as Nellie and her boyfriend, Leigh Thompson, did, Jessie and Ridley often walked hand-in-hand on the Tennessee Centennial Celebration grounds during the six exciting months the exposition was open – from May through October 1897. The Tennessee Centennial was the most exotic place the young people had ever seen.

At the Centennial, over meals at Maggie Bond's boarding house and other places, Ridley gradually learned about Jessie's family. Although

Jessie was born in Nashville, her two older sisters, Mamie and Nellie, were born in Shelbyville, her mother's hometown. Her parents were married in Shelbyville on February 20, 1866, only nine months after Jesse had signed an oath of allegiance to the United States and was "duly released" from Rock Island Prison.

Jesse Ely had grown up in Clarksville – one of three sons and five daughters of Jesse and Charlotte Ely. Mr. Ely was in the hat business in Clarksville where he had moved as a young man from Logan County, Kentucky, where his parents and Ely grandparents lived.[10] The hat store that Mr. Ely and Joshua Brown owned and operated was the first exclusive hat store in Clarksville's history and was very successful, largely because Ely and Brown were "men of untiring energy, industry and unflinching integrity." In time, Mr. Ely was able to build a comfortable house on the Charlotte Road, later renamed Greenwood Avenue, for his large family. After moving there, he rented out their former house in town, bringing him additional income.

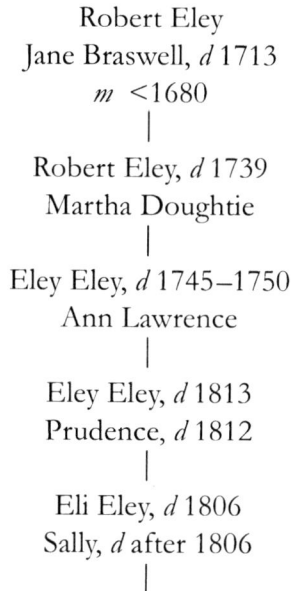

Robert Eley
Jane Braswell, *d* 1713
m <1680
|
Robert Eley, *d* 1739
Martha Doughtie
|
Eley Eley, *d* 1745–1750
Ann Lawrence
|
Eley Eley, *d* 1813
Prudence, *d* 1812
|
Eli Eley, *d* 1806
Sally, *d* after 1806
|

---

10   Jesse Ely was born February 12, 1802 in Logan County, Kentucky, the son of Eli and Sally Ely, and the grandson of Eley and Prudence Eley, all of whom lived in Logan County, although born in Virginia or North Carolina.

Jesse Ely (1803–1847)
Charlotte Jamison (1809–1875)
m 1830

|

Jesse Ely, Jr. (1837–1897)
(1) Ruth Whiteside (1844–1873)
m 1866
(2) Mary Whiteside Mitchell (1837–1893)
m 1874

Under the careful training of their mother, the Ely children would all grow to become "honorable, influential members of society." Edward B. and William J. Ely would be particularly prominent in late 19th century Clarksville. Edward would become the city's leading confectioner and baker, as well as serving as a director of the First National Bank. William J., a Confederate veteran, would become a partner in the People's Warehouse. Earlier, he was a partial owner of the Elephant Warehouse. In 1897, William would be elected Grand Commander of the Clarksville Masonic Lodge. For decades, the Elys were influential members of the Baptist Church.

Jesse Ely, Jr. with his sisters

The author of *Picturesque Clarksville* wrote "That denomination owes much to the unceasing zeal and support of the Ely family." In 1857, when young Jesse Ely, Jr. was 20 years old, he moved to Nashville to enter the dry goods business, having gained valuable experience by working in his father's store in Clarksville.

Four years later, the Civil War broke out. Enthralled with the excitement of secession that permeated Nashville, Jesse, then 23 and unmarried, volunteered for service in Company B, The Rock City

Guards,[11] First Tennessee Infantry Regiment on May 2, 1861. The regiment of Nashville boys went by train to Camp Harris in Alisona, Tennessee, before moving to Camp Cheatham, six miles from Springfield on the Edgefield and Kentucky Railroad.

On July 10, 1861, Jesse Ely and the First Tennessee Regiment were ordered to go to Virginia. They reached Nashville the next afternoon and were entertained on the grounds of the Nashville Female Academy before leaving for Virginia that night. After being sidetracked at Johnson City for a week, they took the cars, on July 21, for Lynchburg, Charlottesville and Staunton where they camped for a week. Later that month they joined the 7th Tennessee under Col. Robert Hatton and the 14th under Col. W.A. Forbes, forming Anderson's Brigade of Loring's Division of Robert E. Lee's Army of the Northwest. After strenuous marches in the mountains, the First Tennessee went into winter quarters before making a long march down the Valley to Winchester, Va., where they arrived on December 28.

While at Winchester, Ely and the others heard of the fall of Fort Donelson. Almost immediately, the First Regiment was ordered to report to Gen. Albert Sidney Johnson, then in command of the Army of Tennessee. Leaving Winchester on February 17, 1862, they finally reached Corinth, Mississippi, by rail on April 7, 1862, too late to fight at Shiloh. Following General Johnston's death, General Beauregard assumed command of the Army of Tennessee. He soon relinquished command to Gen. Braxton Bragg.

On August 28, 1862, Bragg's Army of Tennessee crossed the Tennessee River in route to its Kentucky campaign that lasted until late October. Once, during that campaign, after a tiring march, Jesse and other members of Company B lay down and immediately fell asleep along the road only to be awakened to let some general pass. "Jesse Ely cursed the general worse than Noah cursed Ham," recalled Sam Watkins of Company H.

At Perryville, Ely was wounded. He recovered and fought in the battles of Stones River, Chickamauga and Missionary Ridge. While out

---

11   Rock City was a nickname for Nashville in 1861. This came about because the city was largely built on limestone rock.

with a signal corps on Signal Mountain, he was captured on December 16, 1863, and, along with other captured Confederate soldiers, spent a cold and sleepless night under guard at Chattanooga's Union Depot, where there was no fire. Because Chattanooga was under Confederate siege, the Federals escorted the prisoners, including Jesse, on a one-day march to Bridgeport, Alabama, where they were put on Federal gunboats and taken on a two- or three-night trip by river to Rock Island, Illinois, where, upon arriving at midnight, they were put in Rock Island Prison on an island in the Mississippi River. Jesse lived in a barrack built of rough boards 20 feet wide and 80 feet long. He slept in a bunk about three and one-half feet long. The bunks were tiered three bunks deep along each wall. Jesse and the other prisoners received regular army rations. Each barrack elected its own orderly who managed the commissary and business affairs.

About six months later, Jesse was selected with two other prisoners, Joseph H. Warner of Chattanooga, the uncle of Percy and Edwin Warner of Nashville, and Walter Porter of South Carolina, to work in Adjutant Higgs' headquarters office. This happened because, before the war, Warner had befriended Higgs in Nashville. The new jobs entitled the three young Confederates to better quarters and privileges of the island. It also isolated them from the smallpox infection that was spreading through the prison barracks, and may have saved their lives. During this almost pleasant interlude, Jesse drew a sketch of the prison using tobacco juice and vegetable dyes. It would be later given to his daughter, Charlotte Ely "Lol" Nelson. She made color copies of the drawing for other family members, including my father, Jesse Ely Wills. I have enjoyed having one of those copies for decades. Only in recent years when, by chance, I discovered Joseph H. Warner's reminiscences of Rock Island prison[12] that mentioned Jesse Ely, did I understand how my great grandfather got outside the prison gates to paint the prison from that perspective. Ely, Porter and Warner were sent back inside the prison when an order came from the War Department to return the prisoners to the barracks. Warner also wrote that, at some point

---

12   *Chattanooga Regional Historical Journal*, Volume 9, number 2, December 2006, "Personal Glimpses of the Civil War," J.H. Warner, pp. 33-34.

Drawing of Rock Island Prison by Jesse Ely

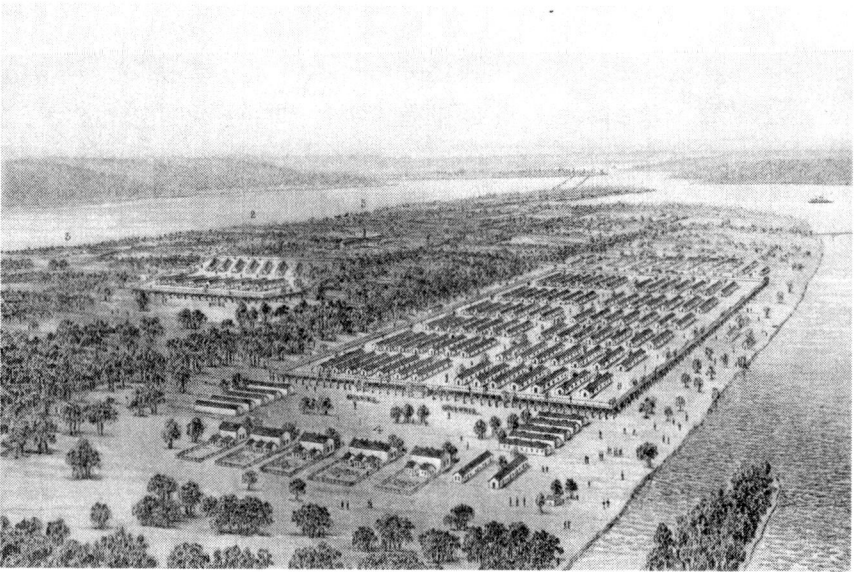

Prison Barracks and Hospital, Rock Island, Illinois

21

during his imprisonment at Rock Island, Secretary of War Edwin M. Stanton issued a directive authorizing Confederate prisoners at Rock Island to enlist in the U.S. Army for one year. Those who volunteered to do so were to be given a $100 bounty and paid $8 a month. They were promised that they would not have to fight Confederates but would instead be sent west to fight the Indians. Jesse declined and remained in prison until the end of the war. When he signed the oath of allegiance on May 14, 1865, he listed his complexion, hair and eyes as dark. Jesse was five feet, eight inches tall and 24 years old. He was ready to put the war behind him.

Ridley was fascinated with Jessie's wartime stories about her father because his father, Dr. William Thaddeus Wills, also was in the Army of Tennessee and participated in the Kentucky campaign and the battles at Shiloh, Chickamauga and Missionary Ridge in which Jesse Ely fought. Ridley wondered if his dad might have treated Jesse when he was wounded at Perryville.

At various times, Jessie and her sisters told Ridley more about their family. Jessie said that, after her parents married, her mother, Ruth, continued to live with her parents, Thomas Cooper Whiteside, whom his daughters called "Pa," and Margaret Whiteside, and some of her nine siblings in their beautiful, two-story brick home with a classical Greek portico and Ionic columns. The house was on the Murfreesboro turnpike less than a mile north of the Shelbyville public square.[13]

While his wife remained in Shelbyville, Jesse returned to the dry-goods business in Nashville, boarding at first at the St. Charles Hotel on North Market Street and later at 43 S. Cherry Street. Initially, he worked for R.H. Thompson, who sold men's furnishing goods, hats and caps at 41 N. Cherry Street. On weekends, Jesse would take the Friday evening train to Shelbyville before returning to Nashville Sunday night. By 1870, Jesse and Ruth had two little girls, Nellie and Mamie. Ruth regularly wrote Jesse how the girls were progressing. In a March 10, 1871, letter, she spoke of Nellie and Mamie having the nettle rash and added, "Nellie wants to play the piano all the time." By 1871, Jesse had bought out Mr. Thompson and started his own dry-goods business with

---

13   The Thomas Cooper Whiteside home, long neglected, was razed in 2008.

Ruth's brother, Tom Whiteside Jr. By this time, Jesse had moved again, to 73 N. High Street, a house large enough to accommodate his growing family, At this point, Ruth and their little girls moved to Nashville from Shelbyville. The next year, on September 11, 1871, Jesse and Ruth had a third daughter, Jessie. There, 19 months later, Ruth Whiteside Ely died of complications three days after giving birth to another little girl, whom Jesse named for her. Baby Ruth lived only a few months.

Jesse knew that his young daughters needed a mother so he courted and married Ruth's widowed sister, Mary E. Whiteside Mitchell. This was a practice that was common in the nineteeth century. With her help raising the children, Jesse could turn his full attention to the store on North Cherry Street where he and Whiteside Jr. were partners. They continued this active partnership until Tom moved to Chattanooga. He would die in 1879, when he was 32.

By 1875, Whiteside's name had come off the storefront. Henceforth, the business was known as Jesse Ely's Store. Ely changed his merchandise according to the seasons and took advantage of promotional opportunities. Early each spring, he marked down all his winter offerings, closing them out at low prices to make way for his spring style silk and cashmere hats. Soon, light-colored stuff and straw hats would replace them. In October 1887, when President and Mrs. Grover Cleveland visited Belle Meade, Ely sold top hats with Cleveland's likeness on the hatband. In November 1889, he was selling winter underwear, camel's-hair shirts and drawers, Derby ribbed shirts and drawers, and Scotch wool shirts and drawers.

In the summers, Mary and Jesse felt it was important for her to take their daughters out of the hot, crowded city. Invariably, they took the train to Shelbyville to stay with the girls' grandmother in the wonderful house they all loved. Mary did this one August when Nellie had "two little teeth and 12 or 13 boils on her legs," and Mamie was having trouble with her bowels. She suggested that Jesse come down on the Saturday morning train and bring her "ten yards of domestic." By this time, Mrs. Whiteside was growing frail.

Fortunately, the Ely girls were grown or nearly so when Mary Whiteside Mitchell Ely died in February 1893 after an illness of several weeks. Prayers were said at the Ely residence on Tuesday the 14th led by the Rev. Jerry Witherspoon, minister of First Presbyterian Church. That evening, Mrs. Ely's remains were taken by train to Shelbyville. The funeral took place at the home of her widowed mother, Margaret Ann Robinson Whiteside, the next afternoon. Her obituary noted, "Mrs. Ely was beloved by a wide circle of friends in the community of her girlhood and to that neighborhood to which she afterward removed." She was buried beside her first husband, Capt. Thomas R. Mitchell, on the Whiteside lot in Willow Mount Cemetery next to the large Confederate plot.

While he was courting Jessie, Ridley gradually learned how prominent so many of her ancestors were. He was intrigued about the probability that Jessie was descended from Gen. Evan Shelby (1720-1794), who came to America with his parents, Evan and Catherine Daviess Shelby, before 1754 from Wales. The younger Evan Shelby married Letitia Cox. Interested in the Indian trade, he became involved in trading posts and was in General Braddock's campaign in 1755, when Shelby laid out part of the road from Frederick, Maryland to Fort Cumberland. Two years later, he was commissioned by Governor Sharpe of Maryland as captain of a company of rangers. He also held a commission as captain of a Pennsylvania militia company. Shelby was in the advance party under Gen. John Forbes that took possession of Fort Duquesne in 1757, having first crossed the Ohio River with more than half of his scouts to make a reconnaissance of the fort. With John Sevier, Shelby led the over-mountain men to their victory over the British at King's Mountain, providing momentum for America to win the Revolutionary War.

The Shelby connection came through Jessie's grandmother, Charlotte Jamison (1809-1875), of Clarksville, who married Jessie's grandfather, Jesse Ely, in 1830. Their first child was Eleanor Shelby Ely named for Charlotte's mother, Eleanor Shelby Jamison. Charlotte Jamison Ely had a brother, David Shelby Jamison. His middle name also supports the argument that their mother's parents were Evan Shelby Jr. and Catherine Shelby, daughter of Dr. John Shelby, of Nashville. Indians killed Evan near Clarksville in 1793 when he was 39 years old. His daughter Eleanor Shelby married William Caldwell Jamison, of Clarksville. His brother, Isaac Shelby, became the first governor of Kentucky and the man for whom Shelby County, Tennessee, was named. Despite exhaustive

24

research the father-daughter relationship between Evan Shelby, Jr. and Eleanor Shelby Jamison has never been proved. Family tradition and circumstantial evidence argue that the line is correct.

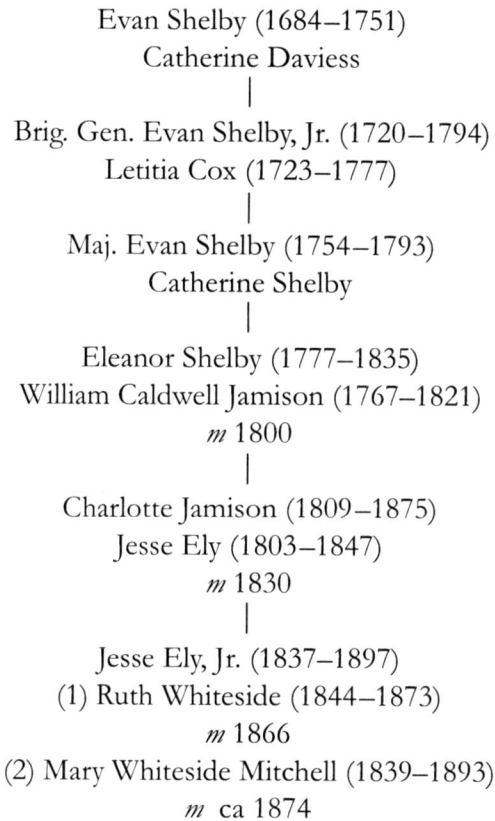

Evan Shelby (1684–1751)
Catherine Daviess
|
Brig. Gen. Evan Shelby, Jr. (1720–1794)
Letitia Cox (1723–1777)
|
Maj. Evan Shelby (1754–1793)
Catherine Shelby
|
Eleanor Shelby (1777–1835)
William Caldwell Jamison (1767–1821)
m 1800
|
Charlotte Jamison (1809–1875)
Jesse Ely (1803–1847)
m 1830
|
Jesse Ely, Jr. (1837–1897)
(1) Ruth Whiteside (1844–1873)
m 1866
(2) Mary Whiteside Mitchell (1839–1893)
m ca 1874

The Whiteside lineage is well documented. Jessie remembered her grandmother, Margaret Ann Robinson Whiteside, as the old lady did not die until 1894, when Jessie was 22. As a girl, Jessie often took the train to Shelbyville to visit her. Mrs. Whiteside was born in Knoxville July 5, 1821. Her parents were Mary Dardis and James Robinson. James was born in Ireland before immigrating to America where, in Knoxville, he married Margaret's mother, Mary Dardis, on August 3, 1820. Mary, who was born in Knoxville in 1802 died in Winchester, Tennessee, in 1834 and is buried in the Winchester City Cemetery. Her parents were James and Lucy Sims Dardis. Mr. Dardis was born in Ireland in 1776, while his wife, Lucy, was born in Culpeper County, Virginia, three years later. Dardis, as a 20 year old, fled to America with his two brothers, Thomas and Edward, fugitives from Protestant persecution. Ireland was then ruled by an All-Protestant Parliament. Although Roman Catholics had, by the late part of the 18th century, regained rights to hold land and practice Catholicism, they had no political rights. In the raw community of Knoxville the Dardis brothers and James White, the founder of Knoxville, who was a generation older, knew each other.

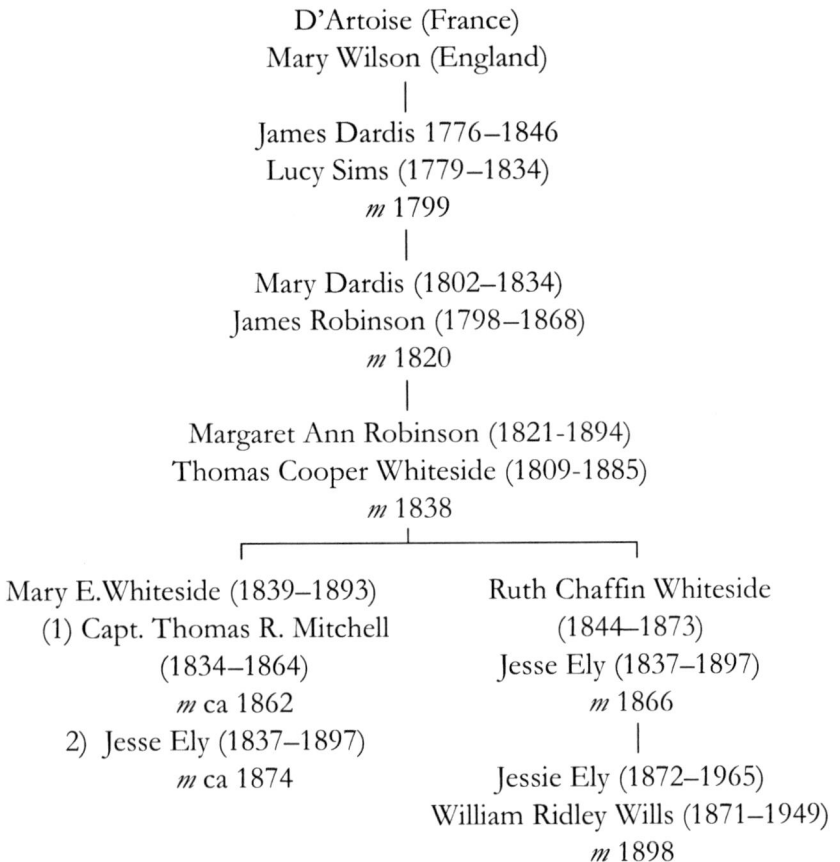

D'Artoise (France)
Mary Wilson (England)
|
James Dardis 1776–1846
Lucy Sims (1779–1834)
m 1799
|
Mary Dardis (1802–1834)
James Robinson (1798–1868)
m 1820
|
Margaret Ann Robinson (1821-1894)
Thomas Cooper Whiteside (1809-1885)
m 1838

Mary E. Whiteside (1839–1893)
(1) Capt. Thomas R. Mitchell
(1834–1864)
m ca 1862
2) Jesse Ely (1837–1897)
m ca 1874

Ruth Chaffin Whiteside
(1844–1873)
Jesse Ely (1837–1897)
m 1866
|
Jessie Ely (1872–1965)
William Ridley Wills (1871–1949)
m 1898

When Gov. William Blount moved the territorial capital to Knoxville in 1793, he and his family lodged with Dardis, who also knew Tennessee's first governor, John Sevier. Like most men on the Western frontier, Sevier was not a member of an organized church. He was, however, influenced in his religious viewpoints by James Dardis. In his journal, Sevier wrote about subscribing to a Washington City newspaper for Dardis. A few days later, Sevier wrote about having attended a "Catholic meeting."

In 1799, Governor Sevier, possibly influenced by Dardis, offered some land in Knoxville for a Catholic settlement to the Rev. Stephen T. Badin, a Catholic priest serving in Kentucky as a missionary. As a matter of fact, Badin was the first Catholic priest to be ordained in the United States. Sevier and Badin did not strike a deal, as Badin thought the price of Sevier's land was too high.

It was not until 1808 that Badin visited Knoxville. Upon arrival, he found six or seven Irish families there and preached four times in the state house, which probably was a tavern. In speaking of his visit, Badin spoke of a "French gentleman" as the "principal Catholic of the place." The late Thomas Stritch, author of *The Catholic Church in Tennessee* and a native Nashvillian, thought it was almost certain that Badin was referring to James Dardis, whose name suggested he might have been French. Badin returned to Knoxville twice more, in 1809 and 1810, to establish a church. He apparently had little success. Father Badin later lived among the Indians in Indiana and was one of the founders of Notre Dame University, where he is buried.

Knoxville's corporate existence began on October 27, 1815, when the State Legislature passed an act incorporating the inhabitants of "the town of Knoxville." About three months later, seven aldermen met for the first time. They constituted the town's first councilmen. One of those councilmen was James Dardis, who administered the oath of office to one of his fellow aldermen, James Park. When Knoxville decided in January 1816 to erect a city market, James Dardis was one of three men who contracted for and supervised the construction of the public building.[14]

---

14   *The American Historical Magazine and Tennessee Historical Quarterly,* vol. VIII, April, 1903, No. 2, p. 183-84.

Dardis balanced his civic duties with his religious interests. In October 1821, he put a notice in the *Knoxville Register* announcing an impending visit by Father Robert Abell and Father Guy Chabrat, Badin's successors in Kentucky. The visit seems not to have materialized, and East Tennessee did not see a priest again for 30 years.

In 1829, James Dardis moved to Winchester, Tennessee, with his wife, Lucy, and and some of their children. Because Franklin County was overwhelmingly Protestant, there was no priest there. On rare occasions, priests did visit the area. On one such visit, a priest recalled that Dardis told him that he never failed to read the prayers for Mass on Sundays, most of the time without the Mass itself. In his book, Thomas Stritch marveled at "the enormous powers of faith, hope, charity and perseverance" that underlaid Dardis' loyalty to Catholicism. James Dardis died in 1846 and was buried in the Winchester City Cemetery. There were always a few Catholics in Winchester after Dardis' death, and the town gradually became a Catholic center of sorts toward the end of the 19th century when the Paulist Fathers came there.

Lucy and James Dardis' daughter, Mary, was born in 1802 in Knoxville. On August 3, 1820, she married 22-year-old James Robinson, who, like her father, was a native of Ireland. They had four children, the oldest of whom was Margaret Ann Robinson, born in Knoxville on July 5, 1821. The Robinsons also moved to Franklin County where Mary Dardis Robinson died in 1834 and was buried in the Winchester City Cemetery on her father's lot. Her husband, James, lived in Winchester until his death in 1868.

On May 24, 1838, the beautiful 17-year-old Margaret Ann Robinson married Thomas Cooper Whiteside, a 27-year-old Protestant attorney, then living in nearby Shelbyville, Tennessee. He was born June 29, 1809, in Chester County, Pa. Thomas came to Tennessee as a youth with his father, David Whiteside (1785-1859) who was influenced to come to Tennessee because David's brother, Jenkin Whiteside, had settled in Davidson County in 1805 and become very successful, serving as U.S. Senator from 1809 until 1811 and wining acclaim as a great criminal lawyer and specialist in land law.

Thomas Cooper Whiteside graduated from The University of Nashville in 1828 and later studied law under John Bell. In 1831, he moved to Shelbyville where he practiced law on the public square. He and Margaret Ann had eleven children – Mary E. (1839), Margaret C. (1840), Henry Clay (1842), Ruth Chaffin (1844), Thomas Cooper, Jr. (1847), James Robinson (1849), David Jenkin (1851), John Finley (1854), Ada C. (1856), Susan A. (1859), and Annie S. Whiteside (1862). Ruth and Mary E. would become the first and second wives of Jesse Ely. Mary's first husband was Capt. Thomas R. Mitchell, C.S.A., who was murdered in Bedford County in December 1864.

Thomas Cooper Whiteside, for many years a leader of the Whig Party in Bedford County, attended the 1848 Whig Convention determined to vote for Henry Clay or Daniel Webster. Seeing no chance for the election of either, he made the seconding speech for Gen. Zackary Taylor, the Mexican War hero. Upon returning home, Whiteside, an earnest and logical, rather than eloquent, public speaker, made many speeches on behalf of General Taylor in the general election campaign. After Taylor's election, Whiteside was urged to accept a position in Taylor's administration. He declined, preferring to practice law in Shelbyville. Later he became a director of the Nashville and Chattanooga Railroad. At his death in 1885, he had served longer as a director of the railroad than any other man. He was also president of the Shelbyville Savings Bank.

During the Civil War, the Whiteside home became a refuge for lonely Confederate soldiers who were attracted by the presence of the Whiteside daughters, In 1862, Margaret (Maggie), who was 22 and Ruth, who was 17, were unmarried and considered "Southern beauties." When their brother, Henry C. Whiteside, was wounded at the Battle of Chickamauga in September 1863, Maggie was given a special escort through the lines to bring her brother back to Shelbyville, where she nursed him back to health. The oldest sister, Mary, was married to Capt. Thomas R. Mitchell, C.S.A., who, in 1863, was stationed in Cleburne's Division at nearby Wartrace. When Confederate forces were forced to evacuate Shelbyville that summer, William F. Carnes, C.S.A., who knew Ruth and Maggie slightly, asked Lt. Ingraham, of Smith's battery, known to be one of Miss Maggie's devoted admirers, if he could help transport the Whiteside sisters, Mary and Maggie, to Tullahoma. Mary said she was quite willing to ride behind an officer on his horse to get away from the Yankees and reach her husband's command. Maggie also wanted to leave. Lt. Carnes found a small horse-drawn ambulance and convinced Dr. Frank Rice, the division surgeon, to let him borrow it to take Mrs. Mitchell and Miss Maggie to Tullahoma, at which point he would return the ambulance. Carnes escorted them, accompanied by Dr. Phillips, another admirer of Miss Maggie, to Tullahoma, where the young women stayed at the house of a friend. Carnes then found Capt. Mitchell and told him where he could find his wife.

On the mild and pleasant winter day of December 6, 1864, Capt. Thomas Mitchell and a fellow Confederate soldier came galloping toward Shelbyville on the Nashville, Murfreesboro and Shelbyville Turnpike. They were headed to the Whiteside house to see Mitchell's wife, Mary, and baby daughter, Maggie. Some miles outside town, they were seen by a band of Union Home Guards who gave chase. About two miles west of Shelbyville on the Fishing Ford Pike, Mitchell and his friend were overtaken by the home guards and, seeing no possibility of escape, surrendered. Disregarding this, the home guards continued firing and shot the 30-year-old Mitchell through the lungs. Leaving him beside the road to die, they rode back to Shelbyville and the Whiteside house, where they knew Mitchell's wife, Mary lived. At the front gate, they yelled for her to come out. When she did, one of the home guard shouted, "You had better send someone out to see about Mitchell. We shot him and left him for dead about two miles from town. You will find him there in a fence corner." Mrs. Mitchell informed her family what had happened and quickly gathered bandages, medicine and liniment and started out to find her husband. On the way, they stopped at Dr. Thomas Lipscomb's house and got him to ride out with them.[15] They found Mitchell still alive but mortally wounded. The next day, he was taken back to the Whiteside house where he died from his wounds on December 9. Other Confederate scouts in the area quickly heard about the murder and sent word to Mary Whiteside Mitchell that they wanted to give him a military burial. At 4:00 p.m. on Sunday, December 10, 1864, Mrs. Mitchell, other family members and a few Confederate scouts surrounded Captain Mitchell's grave in Willow Mount Cemetery for the

---

15   Dr. Lipscomb's daughter, Agnes, married Henry Clay Whiteside in 1866.

Ruth Chaffin Whiteside Ely
(1844–1873)

Jesse Ely
(1837–1897)

service. After taps were sounded and shots fired over the grave, someone alerted the attendees that Yankee soldiers were fast approaching the cemetery. The Confederate soldiers quickly mounted their horses and galloped out to intercept the enemy who turned out to be the same home guard who killed Captain Mitchell. In the skirmish that ensued, one of the eight home guard members was killed.

After Mary's sister, Ruth Whiteside Ely, died in 1873, she married Ruth's former husband, Jesse Ely, and moved to Nashville to be help him rear his daughters. Mary and Jesse Ely had two children, Charlotte who was born in 1876, and William Edward, born in 1878. The little boy died in 1881, but Charlotte would grow up to marry Henry P. Nelson and have three daughters, Mary, Margaret and Louise. The girls would grow up in Atlanta. Unfortunately, Mary Ely died February 13, 1893.[16] She was buried in her hometown of Shelbyville near the remains of her first husband, Captain Mitchell, in the Whiteside lot in Willow Mount Cemetery.

By 1896, Jessie and her sisters were increasingly worried about their dad. He had not been feeling well since the previous winter. In February 1896, Jesse wrote his daughter, Nellie, who was in St. Louis visiting Margaret Mitchell Hagar, who had lived with the Jesse Ely family from the time her mother married Mr. Ely until her marriage in 1888 to William Gardner Hagar, of Plattsburgh, N.Y. The Hagars initially lived in Nashville where they had two children, Thomas Mitchell Hagar, born in 1890, and Mary Whiteside Hagar, born in 1893. Sometime later, Margaret and William Hagar and their children moved to St. Louis, Missouri. They invited Nellie, who was fond of

---

16   *Shelbyville Times-Gazette*, March 8, 1995.

Margaret to visit. In his February 1896 letter, Mr. Ely told Nellie, "I have not been at all well for some weeks but manage to keep up."

In March 1897, Ridley became an uncle. On the third of that month, Mann and Della Wills had their second child, a baby son whom they named William Ridley Wills II, for his uncle Ridley. The baby would be called Ridley. Meanwhile, Jessie's dad's health had continued to deteriorate although he still tried to walk every day to his store where he had, in several locations on Cherry Street, sold gent's furnishing goods, hats and caps at the lowest prices for more than two decades. In the summer, Jesse Ely's health deteriorated to the point that he became bedridden. On September 12, he was stricken with a paralysis, and the next day he fell into a coma. The 60-year-old Nashvillian, who was a Knights Templar, died at home on September 15, survived by his four daughters, and seven brothers and sisters, all of whom lived in their hometown of Clarksville. One brother, William J. Ely, was at the time of Jesse's death, commander of the Freemasons' Clarksville Lodge.

Mary Whiteside Mitchell Ely (1837–1893)

Jessie Ely Wills (1872–1965)

Jesse's daughter, Nellie, who had been planning her wedding to T. Leigh Thompson since the summer, decided to scale back her wedding plans due to her father's death. "It will," she said, "be a quiet wedding. No cards have been issued." Nellie and Leigh married at her home on November 11. Only family members and a few dear friends attended. One of the most prominent politicians in the state, Mr. Thompson, was 35, a veteran of two terms in the state legislature and president of the State Association of Sons of the Confederacy when he married Nellie, who had just celebrated her 27th birthday. The ring bearer and flower girl were little Mitchell and Mary Hagar, of St. Louis. Nellie wore a toilet of white organdy over white silk, simply but prettily made, and carried a

32

William Ridley Wills
(1871–1849)

bouquet of white roses and lilies of the valley A full veil of tulle completed the costume. The Rev. James I. Vance gave the marriage vows under the arch separating the drawing rooms. Governor Taylor and his staff gave the bride and groom a massive silver service. On the silver tray was inscribed "To Col. Nellie Ely Thompson from Gov. Taylor and his staff." Another handsome gift was a chest of silver from the state officials at the State Capitol. After returning from their honeymoon to Washington and other eastern cities, Mr. and Mrs. Thompson lived with her sister, Charlotte and her husband, Henry P. Nelson, at the Ely home until spring. [17]

Jessie and Ridley were also in love. When he proposed in 1898, she accepted on the condition that he always provide for her 31-year-old, unmarried sister, Mamie, whom Jessie thought would never marry. Ridley readily agreed to do so. The marriage took place at high noon on October 19, 1898, at the Ely residence on North Vine Street, where Charlotte (Lol) and Henry Nelson had lived since their marriage. About 50 friends and relatives witnessed the ceremony. Among the guests were Mann and Della Wills of Brownsville; Agnes Lipscomb (Mrs. Henry C.) Whiteside, of Shelbyville; Judge Walter Bearden, and Susan Whiteside (Mrs. Edmund) Cooper Jr., of Shelbyville; Mr. and Mrs. Howard Pettus, Mr. Harry Pickering and one of Jessie's uncles from Clarksville.

For the wedding, the drawing rooms were thrown together and converted into a bower of tropical splendor by palms and potted plants. This was the same room where Nellie married T. Leigh Thompson and where Charlotte married Henry Nelson. The chandeliers were entwined with vines. Amid the wealth of green was a pure white chrysanthemum, the first of the season. The wedding was of elegant simplicity. Rev. James I. Vance, minister of the First Presbyterian Church, performed the ceremony at which there were no attendants. Jessie, who was petite,

17   By 1900, the Nelsons had moved to 2005 Hayes Street. That year, Henry was associated with Nestor & Nelson, fire insurance agents. The Nelsons would move to Atlanta by 1903.

wore the daintiest and loveliest of gowns, fashioned of sheer white organdy. Her hat was of white mull, and she carried bride's roses. After the ceremony, a buffet breakfast was served. Jessie and Ridley left shortly after the ceremony for an Eastern tour. Upon their return they would live at the Maney residence at 1911 Hayes Street.

Early in 1899, Jessie told Ridley that she was pregnant. He was thrilled and was solicitous of her during her pregnancy. Dr. Charles Briggs delivered the baby at the Wills home, on August 31, 1899. They named the baby boy Jesse Ely Wills in memory of Jessie's father.

Three months later, 150 miles to the west in Brownsville, a friend of the Wills, Nellie Halliburton gave birth to a little boy named Richard Halliburton.[18] He would grow up to become an internationally known writer, journalist and lecturer just as Ridley Wills would become a nationally respected life insurance executive. Ridley's aunt, Eva Mann Moore, of Brownsville, was kin to both men, and would have great difficulty in the early and mid-1930s keeping that fact to herself.

---

18   Halliburton swam the Hellespont, the Panama Canal and the Sea of Galilee. He met with headhunters in Borneo and visited Devil's Island Prison. His last great adventure was to sail a Chinese junk with 12 crewmembers across the Pacific. It foundered in heavy seas half way across and he was never heard of after his final dispatch March 24, 1939.

CHAPTER IV

A RISKY MOVE

One day in July 1898, a fine-looking man, wearing a silk hat and a long-tailed coat and carrying a gold-headed cane, made an appointment to see Ridley Wills, deputy insurance commissioner for Tennessee. The man introduced himself as Robert H. Hutchinson. Ridley knew that Hutchinson had a little company with $500 in assets that he had just merged with another small company called the National Sick and Accident Association, run by an Irishman named Michael J. O'Shaughnessy. Mr. Hutchinson told Ridley he wanted to qualify his company as a sick and accident association. Wills told him that $500 would not qualify his company as a sick and accident association. So, instead, Hutcheson said he wanted his company qualified as a fraternal and beneficial order because that did not require him to have a penny. He convinced a skeptical Wills that his was a fraternal order. Wills relented, thinking, if he did not do much good, he wouldn't do much harm. Although Hutchinson changed his company's by-laws to qualify as a fraternal order, he did not comply with other procedures called for. Soon Ridley resigned his position, succeeded by Cornelius A. "Neely" Craig.

Mann Wills
(1870–1936)

On February 23, 1900, Craig, officially notified Col. Robert H. Hutchison that his company did not qualify as a fraternal organization and must change its status either to an assessment association or a legal reserve life insurance company. Mr. Hutchison, who had six employees and a modest office in the Twin

Della Womack Wills
(1874–1953)

Building on Cedar Street, chose to become an assessment association, and invited a young man named C. Runcie Clements to join him as

an incorporator. Runcie accepted and became company president in December 1900 after Mr. Hutchinson died of a heart attack precipitated by a buggy accident in Nashville that threw him to the street and broke his leg. Complications developed and Hutchinson's leg was amputated in a vain attempt to save his life.

At the time Craig notified Mr. Hutchinson that his company would be closed unless it complied with the department's demands, his brother, E. B. Craig, state insurance commissioner, was preoccupied, having been offered a position as treasurer of the newly organized Virginia Iron, Coal, and Coke Company in Bristol, Virginia. Craig delayed giving an answer until he completed his term as state treasurer. He also recommended to the Bristol company officials that they offer his former associate, Ridley Wills, a position as assistant treasurer. The iron, coal and coke executives did so. After talking the opportunity over with Jessie, Ridley took the train to Bristol, where he accepted the offer. As soon as Mr. Craig's term of office expired, he also accepted and moved to Bristol. The *Nashville Banner* took note of Mr. Craig's eight years as State Treasurer and Insurance Commissioner. It said that, "by his selection of able deputies who stared his pride in his administration, the insurance department was built up until it gained a reputation as one of the best conducted in the country, and, at the same time, the state's revenue from the department was doubled."

Craig and Wills soon were joined by their families in Bristol.[19] Confident that they had served the state well in the insurance department, they focused on making the coal company a success. In September, Jessie became pregnant and, on June 11, 1901 delivered a healthy baby girl, whom she named "Mamie" for her beloved sister Mamie Ely. Out of Ridley's and Jessie's friendship with and respect for E.B. and Mamie "Mag" Craig, they gave Mamie a middle name of "Craig." Ridley was pleased that Mamie Craig had a first cousin, Harriette Catchings Wills, Mann and Della's third child, who was only eleven months older than she.[20] When Jessie and Ridley visited Brownsville, the two little girls

---

19   E.B. and Margaret "Mamie" Crockett Craig had four children, Corinne, Margaret "Mamie," Nathaniel "Nate", and Edward B. Jr.

20   Harriette Catchings Wills Oglesby was born August 26, 1900.

became friends. On March 26, 1902, Mann and Della Wills completed their family with the birth of a third little girl. Named Elizabeth for her grandmother Wills, she would grow up to share with her older brother, Ridley, and her first cousin, Jesse, a love of English literature. The four Mann Wills children, Trousdale, Ridley, Harriette, and Elizabeth, all joined the First Presbyterian Church when they each became 10 years old.

On December 15, 1901, Nashville set a new record for low temperature with an official reading of 2.2 degrees below zero. Two days later, the city was blanketed with snow. That afternoon, C.A. Craig read the *Nashville Banner* at his desk in the insurance commissioner's office. He suddenly stared at a notice that stated that, on Friday, December 27, 1901 at noon, 115 shares of the capital stock of the National Sick and Accident Association would be auctioned on the steps of the Davidson County Courthouse. The notice said that L.M. Haralson, the executrix of the estate of R. H. Hutchison, reserved the right to reject all bids. Mr. Craig thought to himself, "Man, this is an opportunity for somebody." Neely had come to two conclusions during his four years with the insurance commission. One was that Tennessee had fewer insurance companies in proportion to the amount of insurance in force than any state in the Union. The other was that there was an exceptional opportunity in Tennessee for any life insurance company, particularly one in the industrial insurance business, provided that it would operate on the basis of putting the interests of its policy owners above those of all other interests. Realizing that he didn't have the money to buy the National Sick and Accident Association, he quickly decided to go to Bristol and talk about the matter over with E.B. and Ridley, and, if they were favorably inclined, invite them to join him in trying to buy the company. Neely packed a bag and took an N.C. & St. L. evening train for Chattanooga where he made a connection with a Southern express train with a Pullman sleeper, headed for Bristol and Washington.

The next day, Neely, E.B. and Ridley thoroughly discussed the possibilities of bidding for the company. Although E.B. and Ridley were enthusiastic about Neely's idea to somehow acquire it, E.B. did not think he could relinquish his position as treasurer, having been with the company less than a year. Nevertheless, he encouraged Ridley to go back to Nashville and join Neely in the effort. Ridley agreed that was exactly what he wanted to do. With that settled, the three men spend some time considering how much money Neely and Ridley would need, where they might get it, and whom else they should invite to participate with them. The name of Newton White, a prosperous Giles County farmer and longtime friend of the Craig family, was brought up. He had been a classmate of E.B.'s at Webb School, and, more importantly, had the financial wherewithal to help them. With 115 shares available and with each having a par value of $100 it was obvious that they would need White or somebody else to lend them between $10,000 and $20,000. Before Neely left Bristol, E.B. pledged to help him any way he could and said he hoped to join the organization later.

Back in Nashville, Neely knew he had little time. He quickly contacted some of the men whose names came up in Bristol. Some were interested; some were not. He also drove down to Giles County to talk to their best prospect – Newton White, whose 900-acre farm on Richland Creek he had always admired. Mr. White listened with interest to Neely's plan before asking how much money he needed. Neely said, "We figure it will take between $12,000 and $20,000, depending on how many other bidders show up at the auction." After a few more questions, Mr. White told Neely: "I believe you boys can make it. I'll sign your note at one of the banks in Nashville for whatever you need, and I'll come up the first of the week to get it worked out."

At noon on December 27, 1901, Neely and Ridley were on the Davidson County Courthouse steps. With them was a close friend of Neely's, Charles Sykes, a general insurance agent, who had agreed to bid for them. Neely and Ridley quickly spotted their competition. Runcie Clements, president of the association since Hutchinson's death, a director and owner of eleven shares of stock, was there with his brother, R. Marvin Clements; his brother-in-law, H.M. Moore; Ed Kleeman, a young bookkeeper at Lusky and Lowenheim Jewelry Store where Runcie once worked; and Herman Lusky, one of the owners of the jewelry store.

At noon, Miss Lena Haralson, executrix of the estate of Mr. Hutchinson, pounded her gavel and opened the bidding; she decided to sell all 115 shares in one block. As the bidding swapped back and forth between Clements and Sykes, the tension seemed almost visible. When Sykes bid $150 a share, Clements conferred with Mr. Lusky before declining to bid further. Sykes had acquired the 115 shares for $17,250 – only 25 cents a share higher than Clements' final bid. Had Clements bid once more, Neely and Ridley would have folded, having previously decided that $150 a share was as much as they could afford.

On December 30, 1901, the *Nashville Banner* carried two stories of interest to the business community. One was the announcement that C.A. Craig had resigned as deputy insurance commissioner, a position he had held for about a year. He would be replaced by Charles P. Wofford of Memphis. The article said, "Craig has filled this position with credit to himself and to the benefit of the Department and the State, and Treasurer [Reau] Folk parts with him with no little regret and reluctance." The other story revealed that Charles Sykes had purchased control of the National Sick and Accident Association for the benefit of a group composed of C.A. Craig, C.J. Hebert and T.J. Tyne of Nashville; Newton H. White of Pulaski; and W.R. Wills of Bristol.

At some point, Mann Wills had an opportunity to join the National Sick and Accident Association. The family tradition is that three men, presumably Ridley, Neely Craig and Runcie Clements, came to Brownsville and asked Mann if he wanted to invest in and become active in the company. He supposedly told them that he would not think of it as he was making $11,000 a year and that was "big money."

At a National Sick and Accident Association convention at the Duncan Hotel in early January, seventy-five people attended, including Gov. Benton McMillin; Reau E. Folk, state treasurer and insurance commissioner; Edgar Jones, president of Union Bank and Trust Co.; and company representatives. As president of the association, Clements presided. In his remarks, Commissioner Folk congratulated the company on acquiring the management skills of Mr. Craig and Mr. Wills. As the final speaker of the evening, Mr. Clements introduced Mr. Craig, who, he said, would be elected president of the association at a meeting of stockholders and directors within a few days. Mr. Craig spoke of the principles that would govern the association's operations, including putting the policy owners' interests above all other considerations. He also assured the field men present that the new management would be attentive to their needs and understanding of their problems.

The stockholders meeting took place January 7, 1902. At the meeting, all the company's capital stock was represented. Craig and Wills held the 115 shares just purchased. Runcie Clements held 15 shares, the 11 he already owned and four shares he acquired from members of his group. Miss Haralson owned 20 shares and held a proxy for 50 more owned by A.A. and Mary Polis, of Birmingham, Alabama. The stockholders unanimously elected five directors – C.A. Craig, W.R. Wills, T.J. Tyne, N.H. White, and C.J. Hebert. The wild card was Hebert, whose firm, C.J. Hebert and Co., had its offices in the same building at 421 Union St. where the National Sick and Accident Association was. He owned no stock in the company, had no role in its organization and was not re-elected the following January. It is not known why he was named a director. Officers elected were C.A. Craig, president; W.R. Wills, secretary and treasurer; Thomas J. Tyne, general counsel; and C. Runcie Clements, assistant secretary and treasurer. Craig and Wills realized earlier that if their new company was going to be successful, they badly needed the services of Runcie Clements, whom they both liked. He accepted Craig's offer to stick with the company and became invaluable. His first contribution was to quickly wind up the 1901 record and complete the association's annual report. It was said that, in the company's earliest years, Runcie wrote out policies by hand.

Although they may not have been fully aware of it at the time, Neely Craig and Ridley Wills, the principal founders of National Life, complemented each other beautifully. While both men were ambitious, energetic and able, their natures were different. Craig tended to be serious. He had a high sense of morality and a gift for expressing it in words. He often spoke of the ideals and objectives of the company and coined slogans that defined the company for decades to come. Ridley seemed to have an, instinctive understanding of the insurance business and a mathematical mind. He liked people, and people liked him. He was informal and friendly, and he had a sense of humor. A good speaker who seldom used notes, Ridley was known to pace when he talked.

Thomas J. Tyne, general counsel, had gotten to know Neely Craig and Ridley Wills when he represented the National Sick and Accident Association in legal dealings with the Tennessee Insurance Commission.

They were impressed with him then and were impressed that he had worked tirelessly in representing the Tennessee Centennial Celebration with its legal work a few years earlier. A native Nashvillian, he was a product of the city's public and parochial schools, the University of the South and Vanderbilt Law School. For a time, Tyne practiced law in partnership with Pat Mann Estes, a distant cousin of Ridley's and a future general counsel of the Life and Casualty Insurance Company of Tennessee. Tyne, who was married to the former Jane Ratterman of Nashville, was, according to Jesse Wills, "a very charming and cultured gentleman, the highest type of Irishman."

One of the first priorities of the new management group was to acquire control of the 50 shares of National Sick and Accident Association stock owned by Mr. and Mrs. Polis. They accomplished this at a January 20, 1902, board meeting. At the same time, Miss Lena Haralson, having decided to leave the employ of the association, offered her 20 shares for sale. Because the company declined to buy her stock, they were made available to individual members associated with the new management group. On February 13, Tom Tyne bought 10 of those shares, Dr. Rufus Fort, who would soon be named the association's new medical director, bought five shares, and Frank Eaton, a friend of Edward B. Craig from Bristol, bought the other five. Miss Haralson would go on to become an original investor of the Life and Casualty Insurance Company of Tennessee when she, A.M. Burton, Guilford Dudley and Dr. J.C. Franklin founded the company in 1903. She became secretary, a position she would hold for some time.

Rufus Fort, M.D., was an outstanding Nashville physician and surgeon – a man of strong character and very positive convictions. A native of Robertson County, he attended the University of the South and graduated from Vanderbilt Medical School. After completing internships in New York City, Rufus returned to Nashville where he served as surgeon at the Tennessee State Prison in 1895 and as superintendent of Nashville's City Hospital two years later. He was still surgeon there when he was named medical director of the National Sick and Accident Association and a member of its board of directors on January 20, 1903. This was legally possible because, at the same meeting, the stockholders changed the by-laws to increase the number of directors from five to seven. C.J. Hebert was not reelected. The three new directors were Runcie Clements, E.B. Craig, and Dr. Fort. Craig was elected vice-president, although he would not become an active officer in the company until late in his life.

Because his company duties as medical director did not require his full attention, Fort continued his private practice of medicine, which included operating his own sanitarium on the west side of North Vine Street just above Church Street. A bachelor when the new company was founded, Fort would marry Elizabeth Clark of Boston in 1909. Similarly, Tom Tyne continued to practice law with his partner Ernest Pillow after becoming general counsel of National Sick and Accident.

Ridley went back to Bristol temporarily in January to train his successor at Virginia Iron, Coal and Coke. He and Jessie also had to move back to Nashville and find a suitable home for themselves and their children, Jesse and Mamie Craig. The Wills bought a one-story house with a Mansard roof at 1911 Broad St., just down the street from Tarbox School that most of the school-age white children in the western side of town attended. The lot fronted 50 feet on Broad Street, extended south 161.7 feet' to Division Street and was identified on the deed as lot #5 in J.W. Lawless' subdivision.

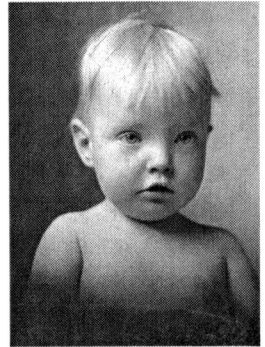

Mamie Craig Wills
1902

There was excitement in Nashville in September 1904 when young Dan McGugin, a famous guard on Fielding Yost's "point a minute" Michigan football teams of 1901 and 1902, arrived in Nashville to coach Vanderbilt. The *Nashville American* and *Nashville Banner* sportswriters acclaimed his methods as the best they had ever seen and forecast future champions. Ridley loved football, became an ardent student of the game and held season tickets every year for the home games played on Dudley Field at the southwest corner of what is now 21st Avenue North and West

Jessie Ely Wills holding her son
Jesse Ely Wills, 1899

End Avenue.

On fall weekends in 1904, Ridley and Jessie would walk to the wooden Vanderbilt stadium where, with the Craigs and other friends, they watched ace halfbacks Dan Blake and John "Honus" Craig lead the Commodores to an undefeated season, scoring 452 points to 4. In 1905, for the second consecutive year, no Southern team scored against Vanderbilt. The highlight of the season came when Vanderbilt traveled to Ann Arbor to play Yost's Michigan team, the greatest football team in the world, undefeated for four seasons. Vanderbilt showed great pluck and determination, losing 18-0. They were handicapped by the absence of their coach, Dan McGugin, who had to go to Tingley, Iowa, that Saturday because of an illness in his family. Still, Vanderbilt was supreme in the South with many newspapers selecting the entire starting 11 as All Southern. Ridley was hooked on Vanderbilt football and would have reserved seats for more than 30 years. One fall, he got so excited at a Vanderbilt game that he accidentally lit the bunting with his cigar.

CHAPTER V

MOVES AND GROWING CHILDREN

In 1904, National Life changed its name to the National Life and Accident Insurance Company, having earlier in the year expanded its operations into Virginia and Mississippi. Because the company was growing rapidly, the home office moved again, in 1905 or 1906, from the Arcade, where the company had been located since 1904, to one entire floor of the five-story Vanderbilt Building on Fifth Avenue North. Later, this monolithic stone structure would be known as the Chamber of Commerce Building.

Not completely satisfied with their house on Broad Street, Jessie and Ridley put it on the market after finding, in February 1906, a home they liked better. The house they selected faced 50 feet south on Patterson Street and extended north 170 feet to an alley. Described as lot number 25, Black's subdivision B in Murphy's Addition, Wills bought the house for $6,541.45 from H.M. and Gertrude DuBose. He paid $1,853.06 in cash and assumed a mortgage of $4,687.79 for the house in the fashionable new subdivision that the Murphy Land Company was developing north of Church Street and south of St. Thomas Hospital. The Wills' new address was 2216 Patterson Street Mr. Wills had no trouble selling his old house on Broad. L. Jonas purchased it in March 1906 for $2,600.21

Wanting to broaden the company's opportunities through health and accident protection in larger amounts on monthly, quarterly, semi-annual and annual premium payments, the company opened a Special Occupation Department in January 1906. Charles P. Wofford, who had succeeded C.A. Craig as deputy insurance commissioner in 1901, joined the company as a director and vice president to run the new department. Because National Life would not employ a trained actuary for some years, Wills usually calculated premium rates. Only when he ran into something he could not handle did the company bring in a professional actuary on a contract basis. Unfortunately, the Special Occupation Department, which had its own field force, did not make money. Excessive claims

---

21   Davidson County Deeds, Book 330, Page 26.

and liberal underwriting standards caused losses of $7,000 in 1907 and slightly less in 1908.

In the fall of 1906, Mrs. Wills took her shy son, Jesse, to first grade at Tarbox School at 1900 Broad Street, where he would stay through the eighth grade. Quickly, Jesse proved to be an excellent student and a child who learned, at an early age, a love of reading. Jesse's little sister, Mamie Craig, entered Tarbox two years later. Miss Emma Kirkpatrick was her first-grade teacher.

Ridley and Mann Wills' mother, Elizabeth "Lizzie" Mann Wills, widow of the late Dr. William Thaddeus Wills, died at her home on Factory Street in Brownsville at on October 19, 1907. She was only 59. Ridley and Jessie drove down to the funeral with their close friends, Neely and Margaret "Mag" Craig. Mrs. Wills was buried in section 3-29 of Oakwood Cemetery near the graves of so many of her Wills and Mann family members. *The Brownsville States-Graphic* wrote of her, "Extensively known and connected, she was from childhood beloved by all with whom she was thrown and her death will be universally regretted. An invalid for many years, she bore her sufferings with Christian fortitude and resignation and met death without a fear. The collection of flower offerings with which the grave was banked was the largest and most beautiful ever witnessed at a burial of an old person in Brownsville."

Mrs. Wills left her heirs, Mann and Ridley Wills as co-owners of four tracts of land in Haywood County: 300 acres of land in the 9th Civil District; 150 acres on Smith Mill Road adjoining land on the south owned by Mann Wills, and by Smith Mill Road and land owned earlier by Asa Mann on the east; the lot in Brownsville where Mrs. Wills lived at the time of her death, bounded by Short Street, Burton Street, Factory Street and Kinney and Freeman Streets; and a half-acre lot in Brownsville bounded by Kinnard, Drake, Taylor and an alley.

In November, Ridley bought Mann's half interest in the 300-acre farm in the 9th Civil District and sold to Mann his half interest in the other three tracts, including the house where their mother had lived.

Despite the loss of his mother, Ridley intended to come back to Brownsville, where his brother lived, as often as possible. Jessie, who found Brownsville to be less sophisticated than Shelbyville, did not relate well to Mann's family. Consequently, she planned to come only when necessary. She and Ridley soon had a happier milestone to celebrate. They went to Clarksville in January to help Jessie's aunt, Eleanor Shelby Ely Pittman, and her husband, Michael Collins Pittman, celebrate their fiftieth wedding anniversary.

T. Leigh Thompson with Jesse and Mamie Craig Wills, c 1906

Wills made a secretarial change in 1909. On May 10 of that year, he hired Miss Margaret Crecelius as his secretary. She would work for him for 27 years, until his breakdown in 1936. During parts of the first four decades of the twentieth century, Crecelius handled Wills' business and private correspondence.

When the Special Occupation Department at National Life continued to struggle in 1909, it became clear that a managerial change was needed. Mr. Wofford resigned and, on September 1, T. Leigh Thompson joined the company as general manager of the department, which soon was called the Ordinary Health and Accident Department. Ironically, Leigh had succeeded Wofford once before. When Wofford resigned as Deputy Insurance Commissioner in 1903, Leigh took his place. By 1911, Thompson had turned the department around. Most of this time, the home office was on the seventh floor of the Stahlman Building at the corner of Third Avenue North and Union Street.

An outstanding event in the early history of National Life came early in 1911 when the company purchased its own home office in downtown Nashville. The company paid Mr. and Mrs. James O. Leake $60,000 for their two-story house, with basement and attic, on the northeast corner of Seventh Avenue North and Union Street. Because National Life was growing so fast, having expanded in its first decade to Georgia (1907), Louisiana (1907), Arkansas (1908), and Kansas (1911), it would soon outgrow the building. In 1912, the company sent Old Guard member W.H. Julian to Dallas to open operations in Texas. After the company began doing business in Oklahoma early in 1913, a contract was let for

46

a $20,000 addition to the crowded home office building at 302 Seventh Avenue North.

Ridley may have gone to Brownsville in November 1911 when Hattie Womack, Della Womack Wills' sister, married Richard Thornton, the oldest of the Thornton boys. Ten months later, Fannie Womack, the third sister, married Richard's younger brother, Macon Thornton. Hattie and Fannie's father, George W. Womack, had moved to Brownsville sometime earlier from Mississippi as his oldest daughter, Della Wills, had lived there for 14 years.

While the Wills were living on Patterson Street, their children continued to attend Tarbox School at 800 Broad St. Later, Mamie Craig would go to Miss Annie Allison's Girls Preparatory School, which opened in 1911. Miss Annie's School or GPS, as it was also called, began in a house at 113 23rd Ave. S., a few blocks from the Wills' home and even closer to Louise Avenue, where the Wills would move in 1914. The school was considered a proper one for the children of genteel families. From its beginning, it featured small classes and intimate contact between Miss Annie and her charges. GPS also emphasized physical exercise, good breathing and good posture. As was common in those days, Miss Annie was both an administrator and a teacher. Her favorite high school classes were French, Latin and English. In 1917, she moved her school to a house at 207 23rd Avenue North.

When Jesse and Mamie Craig were young, their Aunt Nell took them Christmas shopping every year. Jesse and Mamie Craig loved to see the Christmas decorations and gifts, particularly in Phillips and Buttorff's windows. They also carefully picked out, with Aunt Nell's help, Christmas presents for their parents. Jesse recalled that he picked out his first Christmas gift for his mother, without Nell's help, when he was 13. He selected a picture from Stief's Jewelry Company. In the summers, Aunt Nell sometimes treated Jesse and Mamie Craig to ice cream at Paul and John Stumbs' soda fountain at the corner of Fourth Avenue North and Church Street. Another treat was to stop at Mitchell's Candy Store at 323 Union Street.

Ridley and Jessie took their children to the circuses when they came to town. Although Nashville had a zoo at Glendale Park, it was small and could not match the excitement of the circus with its tent full of lions, tigers, bears, hyenas, monkeys and, at least once, a hippopotamus. Jesse was particularly fascinated by the pageantry of the parade that always preceded the appearance of the circus. Uncle Leigh and Aunt Nell would take him and his little sister to Broadway to watch the parade on its way from Union Station to the circus grounds across 25th Avenue North from Centennial Park. That area, which was open land with a creek running through it, was called the commons. Once, when Jesse was entranced by Buffalo Bill Cody and his Wild West show, Mamie Craig became frightened by the Indians, and their parents took them home. Jesse remembered being bitterly disappointed.

Jesse enjoyed playing in Lick Branch, a sizeable creek that meandered through the fields behind his parents' house. His favorite toy ship, a gray cruiser with two funnels and turrets fore and aft, was driven by a clockwork motor. As a small boy, Jesse would take his dog, Skookum, and the boat to the creek where the boat's spring-driven propeller would drive it across wide pools. On other occasions, he caught crawfish in the creek.

Although Mr. Wills was too busy at National Life to take a summer vacation in 1912, he encouraged Jessie to take Jesse and Mamie Craig, then barely 13 and 11, by Pullman car to Atlantic City and the Eastern seaboard. Young Jesse would never forget watching the Pennsylvania Central Train he was riding in round a long curve in the mountains of Pennsylvania. That trip cemented in Jesse a lifelong love of trains.

During the happy years that the Willses lived on Patterson Street, Ridley continued to travel extensively by automobile to visit district offices. In the early years, Shack Wimbish, who later became the highly successful manager of the Rome, Georgia, district office, drove him. Mr. Wills and Mr. Craig, principal founding officers and close personal friends, devoted much of their time during the company's early years, in overseeing the field force and developing new territory. Ridley, who set up the company's agency system, was never happier and or more inspiring than when he visited with "field men." Usually, while on automobile trips to visit districts in Jackson or Memphis, Tennessee, he would make a quick visit to Brownsville, and he would always have a few silver dollars in his pocket to give to children. Occasionally, Ridley and his brother, Mann Wills, whose law office was on the public square in Brownsville, would slip away for a fishing expedition at the camp that Mann's Sunday school class leased at Sunkist Beach adjacent to Reelfoot Lake. While Ridley and Neely were out of town, their associate, Runcie Clements did an excellent job managing home-office operations, including its frequent moves.

When Ridley was home on weekends in the spring, he enjoyed relaxing by watching Vanderbilt baseball practices and games. He also regularly walked for exercise and invited Brownsville students at Vanderbilt over to have dinner or throw horseshoes. One recipient of Wills' hospitality was Samuel Henry Mann Jr., a cousin, who made a stellar record at Vanderbilt, being a member of Delta Kappa Epsilon and Kappa delta Phi legal fraternity. Young Mann also was secretary-treasurer of his class in 1912-13 and 1913-14, business manager of the 1914 *Commodore*, and a member of the track team in 1914. He received his LL.B. degree from Vanderbilt that spring and always appreciated the kindness his cousin, Ridley, paid him while he was in Nashville.

Mr. Wills was a member of the Hermitage Club on Sixth Avenue North, where he entertained friends and business guests. In addition to enjoying excellent meals, each member had a locker, where he could keep bottles of whiskey or scotch. Ridley apparently drank very little, however, and, on Sundays, regularly took his family to worship services at the First Presbyterian Church that he had joined soon after moving to Nashville.

In January 1914, Mann Wills called Ridley to tell him that an older African-American couple in Brownsville, Polk and Tamar Taylor, had asked him to serve as guardian for their grandchildren, both of whose parents had died. If he accepted the responsibility, Mann would be obligated to post a $2,000 bond at the courthouse. He asked Ridley to provide security on the bond. Ridley agreed to do so and, in February, "Mann was duly and regularly appointed guardian for Tamo, Alonzo, Chlave, Opal and Ben Franklin Taylor, minor heirs of Howell Y. Taylor."

With her husband out-of-town much of the time, Jessie was primarily responsible for rearing Jesse and Mamie Craig. She also enjoyed the company of her sisters, Nellie Ely Thompson and Mamie Ely, both of whom lived nearby. Nellie, who later lived on State Street, had no children of her own and consequently doted on her niece and nephew. As was customary in the South for upper-income white families, Mrs. Wills had plenty of domestic help. She employed a cook, a chauffeur, and a yard worker, all Negroes. They either walked to work or rode the electric streetcar, which stopped at the corner of Patterson and 22nd Avenue North. At some point, Mrs. Wills drove an electric automobile, although she never tried driving the more complicated gasoline-powered car. The probability is that she drove a Detroit Electric produced by the Anderson Electric Car Company in Detroit, Michigan. Sold mainly to women and physicians, the Detroit Electric featured a dependable and immediate start without the physically demanding hand cranking of the engine that was required by early internal combustion engine autos. The cars were advertised to reliably get 80 miles between battery recharging.

Mrs. Wills' chauffeur's duties undoubtedly included shopping for or with her at the Farmers Market on the Public Square. Because of having a chauffeur, Jessie never felt handicapped by not being able to drive an internal combustion engine automobile. Many of her friends did not drive and still managed to meet their family, social and civic responsibilities. During World War I, she would be active as a Red Cross volunteer working on the Emergency Canteen Service Committee, as a member of the Executive Committee of the Nashville Chapter of the Fatherless Children of France Society, and as a member of the McCrory Chapter of the D. A. R.

In the summers, Charlotte and Henry Nelson's daughters, Mary, Margaret and Louise, rode the train to Nashville to visit the Willses on Patterson Street. On one such occasion, Margaret and Mamie Craig Wills had their picture taken. Decades later, Elizabeth Wills, who was slightly younger than Jesse, recalled her visits to Patterson Street and later to Louise Avenue. She said that after she, Harriette, Jesse and Mamie Craig would go out in the yard to play,

Jesse and Mami Craig Wills, c 1910

she would soon notice that Jesse had quietly slipped back in the house. When she went in to coax him out again, she would invariably find him stretched out on the floor of the parlor absorbed in reading Cooper's *Leatherstocking Tales*, the works of Scott, Dumas, G.A. Henry or other popular writers. Jesse would look up but usually declined to resume play, preferring to escape by fantasizing himself into stories he had read or imagined. When he was older, Jesse was moved by Herman Melville's *Typee* and *Moby Dick*. Frequently, girlfriends would spend the night with Mamie Craig. One of them, Dot Tucker (Coleman) recalled in 1993 that Mr. Wills was sweet and Mrs. Wills "a little dictatorial but nice." Mamie Craig's closest childhood friend was Helen Hooper, who died prematurely during the 1920s.

The year 1913 was a milestone for the Ridley Wills family. Jessie was proud that her hardworking husband was elected a deacon in the First Presbyterian Church. She hoped that outlet would divert him from the life insurance business, which had become his obsession. And Ridley had much to be pleased about at National Life. Results for the year showed a gain in the company's weekly premium debit of $15,780, greater by 60 percent than for any previous year in the company's history. The young company also achieved a record gain in assets of $256,000. Mr. Wills was by this time widely recognized as one of the foremost authorities in the field of weekly premium insurance in the country.

As the company was prospering and as his salary had increased, Ridley felt comfortable in obtaining a nicer home for his family. According, in June 1913, he purchased two 50' lots on Louise Avenue and began building, at 217 Louise, a handsome, two-story red brick house.[22] He also built, either then or later, a two-story garage for his automobile and as living quarters for the domestic servants. Although Mr. Wills put his house on Patterson Street on the market as soon as his family moved to their new home, it did not sell until February 1920 when Leland L. Dent bought it for $6,500.[23]

Of the Wills' new neighbors on the 200 block of Louise, which

---

22   Davidson County Deed, Book 436, p. 390. The Wills property was bordered by State Street, Louise Avenue, by the Joel Cheeks, and by an alley to the west.

23   Davidson County Deeds, Book 545, page 60.

ran from Church Street north to State Street, the most prominent were Mr. and Mrs. Joel Owsley Cheek, who lived next door at 209. Mr. Cheek was president of the Cheek and Neal Coffee Company and founder of Maxwell House Coffee, a product that would make him a multimillionaire a decade later. Mr. and Mrs. L.S. Frazier lived across and slightly down the street at 212 Louise, while the Hugh F. Kirkpatricks lived at 207 Louise just beyond the Cheeks.[24] These were the only four houses on the block in 1915. On State Street, which ran down the north side of Papa Wills' yard, were the homes of Neely and Mag Craig at 2216; their son, Edwin and his wife, Elizabeth, at 2214; and Runcie and Frances Clements at 2212. Mr. and Mrs. Watkins Crockett lived at 2222 State Street. Next door to them at 2224 State Street were Nell and T. Leigh Thompson. Jesse and Mamie Craig dearly loved their aunt and uncle who were almost like second parents. Mr. Thompson was a Marshall County, Tennessee, native, and a graduate of Webb School and Vanderbilt, where he received a law degree. Before joining National Life, he had served in both the State Legislature and the State Senate before the turn of the century, and he had more recently had been deputy insurance commissioner. Since 1909, Mr. Thompson had continued to run National Life's Ordinary Health and Accident Department, which sold health and accident policies to people who had larger incomes than those who bought the company's weekly premium policies. He would continue to run this department until he retired in 1933 when Mr. Craig, then Chairman of the Board of National Life, paid tribute to his "twenty-four years of loyal and efficient service."

Runcie and Ridley jointly owned the vacant lot on the northeast corner of State Street and Louise Avenue. They felt it was important that this lot not be built on because it was the neighborhood football

---

24   In 1918, Mr. Kirkpatrick died. Soon after that, Mrs. Kirkpatrick's sister and brother-in-law, Dr. and Mrs. Olin West, and their sons, Robert and Olin Jr. moved in with her. Olin West Jr. remembered that Mr. Wills always spoke to him when he was a young boy. He also recalled that, when he was 9 or 10 years old, seeing the Wills' son, Jesse, a Vanderbilt freshman, walk home from the university every afternoon wearing his freshman cap. Although the Wests moved to Chicago in 1922, Olin Jr. returned to live with his aunt from 1926 until 1930 while he was a student at Vanderbilt.

field.[25] One of the boys who played with Jesse there was John Geny, who lived nearby on 22nd Avenue North. Years later, John recalled that one fall, when Jesse didn't have a leather football helmet, he fashioned one out of a cardboard pumpkin, a sure indication that Jesse was something less than a serious athlete.[26]

On balmy evenings, Ridley and Neely often met at the corner of State and Louise after supper and resumed business conversations begun hours earlier at the office. In 1916, as an expression of his friendship, Neely gave Ridley a ring with a ruby inscribed "C. A. C. to W. R. W. 1916." Ridley wore the ring for the rest of his life and, at his death in 1949, his widow, Jessie, gave it to Ridley's namesake and grandson, William Ridley Wills II, who has proudly worn it ever since.[27]

Each Christmas Eve, the Wills and their children, Jesse and Mamie Craig, walked over to the Thompsons' to have supper with Nell, Leigh, and Jessie's unmarried sister, Mary "Mamie" Ely, who was boarding nearby. After eating, the grownups would exchange gifts. Later in the evening, back at home on Patterson Street, Mr. Wills read *The Night Before Christmas* to Jesse and Mamie Craig before they fitfully tried to sleep. On Christmas mornings, the children would open their stockings, which normally contained candies, little toys and novelties – most of which came from Charlie and George Mitchell's Candy and Confectionaries Store. After everyone was dressed, the Wills family would proceed downstairs to open presents that surrounded a red cedar Christmas tree heavily laden with bright ornaments but not with lights because of the threat of fire. A little later in the day, the boys in the neighborhood, including Willie and Bobby Geny, would come by to see Mr. Wills; he traditionally gave each one an agate each Christmas. Sometime over the holidays, Mr. Wills normally drove down to Brownsville for a couple of

---

25   Neighborhood boys played baseball on a somewhat larger vacant lot on the southwest corner of State Street and 22nd Avenue North.

26   Conversation, Ridley Wills II with Bobby Geny, December 3, 1993.

27   There were two family members named William Ridley Wills II. The first was Mann and Della Wills' son, William Ridley Wills II, named for his uncle, Ridley Wills. The second was Jesse and Ellen Wills' son, William Ridley Wills II, named for his grandfather, Ridley Wills.

days to see family members.[28]

In the summers before World War I, Ridley and Jessie took their children on annual vacations by railroad to Atlantic Beach. There, Ridley would stop by a cigar store to buy cigars and the daily *New York Times*. The lifelong Democrat enjoyed reading the newspaper from cover to cover. Consequently, he was perfectly content to settle down in a chair on the boardwalk to enjoy his treats while his wife shopped with their children in the elegant shops along the boardwalk. From their mother, Jesse and Mamie Craig inherited their appreciation for fine jewelry and antiques.

As a boy, Jesse enjoyed reading about railroads and ships. He considered the Pennsylvania as the greatest railroad in the country and compared Penn Station with the Pantheon of Rome in that both were "constructed for the ages." Once he recalled that, while on a overnight train trip to Chicago, he turned out the light in his lower berth, pulled up the shade and watched the fields, trees and houses slide by until the train crossed the Ohio River when he fell asleep. For sheer romanticism, he loved the western streamliners best of all. With their Pullmans, dining cars and observation cars, they possessed glamour that eastern trains had a hard time matching. On their annual trips to Atlantic Beach, Jesse and Mamie Craig would sit on the small platform behind the observation car and listen to the clatter of the wheels as they watched the tracks and telephone poles recede in the distance.

Atlantic City with its Atlantic Ocean stimulated Jesse's lifelong interest in ships. During the First World War, he read every page of the *Scientific American Magazine* to which his father subscribed. Jesse drew, in precise detail, many of the warships illustrated in that publication. His interest in ships began when he read a large illustrated book on the Spanish-American War owned by the husband of a colored maid who worked for his Aunt Nell.

In the fall of 1915, Ridley's nephew, William Ridley Wills II, of Brownsville, entered Vanderbilt. Jessie and Ridley offered him their hospitality, but whether the high-spirited 18-year-old, who had become interested in writing prose and poetry during high school, took advantage

---

28   Letter, Ridley Wills to Jessie Wills, January 12, 1933. Collection of the author.

of their kindness is unknown. His uncle kept up with Ridley, however, and knew he had pledged Alpha Tau Omega Fraternity and was on the *Hustler* staff, a position Ridley would hold during his freshman and sophomore years. Possibly through Mann Wills, Ridley was proud to learn that his nephew was elected president of the Blue Pencil Club in 1915-16, was on the track squad, became editor of the Vanderbilt *Vampire* in 1916, was secretary-treasurer of his sophomore class, was editor of *Flashes* and was on the student council.

While in Vanderbilt, young Ridley wrote a novel based on people he knew in Brownsville. His father paid for publishing the book, which was anything but a hit. When Mann and Della's friends there read it, they easily identified the characters and became quite upset at how Ridley depicted them. For some weeks after the book came out, some friends would cross the street rather than speak to Mr. and Mrs. Wills. Ridley's reaction was," Someday, I will write a bestseller."

In April of Ridley's sophomore year, the United States declared war on Germany. As so many of his classmates did, the idealistic Ridley dropped out of Vanderbilt after school was out and, in the summer of 1917, joined the U.S. Army. His father, Mann, came to Nashville and got him into Col. Luke Lea's regiment so that Ridley would be with boys who were socially his equal. In September, Ridley was first sergeant, Battery B, First Tennessee Artillery at Camp Sevier in Greenville, South Carolina, where he turned down a commission because he felt he was too young to be an officer. Ridley's regiment, renamed the 114th Field Artillery was shipped to France. In late June 1918, Colonel Lea, commander of the 114th, wrote Mann to say he was confident that his men [including Ridley] would "give a splendid account of themselves." Ridley was wounded twice and gassed in France but survived despite the fact that once, when he was gassed, he was not relieved of duty for some time. When the 114th Field Artillery returned to Nashville, Ridley was not with them. He had stayed in France or Germany and would have been charged for being AWOL had not Mann gone to Washington and asked his good friends, Congressman Cordell Hull and Senator Kenneth McKellar, to intercede on his behalf. They did and, in 1919, Ridley came back to New York, received an honorable discharge and, later, a small pension for life.

In May 1917, shortly before Ridley Wills II joined the U.S. Army, a charter was granted to several Nashville citizens to form a local chapter of the American Red Cross. Ridley Wills was one of the original directors. Soon, a canteen committee was organized to distribute fruit, cigarettes, and sandwiches to U.S. Army soldiers on their way to training camps, such as Camp Sevier. Mrs. Ridley Wills and many of her friends, as members of the canteen, spent long hours at Union Station handling these treats from wicker baskets they carried to soldiers who leaned out of the train windows to get them. All the canteen workers wore brimmed hats with a red cross on the front, white aprons with a larger red cross on the front, white stockings and white medium-height heels.

The most traumatic event to take place during Mrs. Wills' Red Cross volunteer work came unexpectedly on the morning of July 9, 1918, when two N.C. & St. L. trains collided at Dutchman's Curve near Belle Meade, killing 101 people, many of whom were African-American workers coming to Nashville to work at the Powder Plant at Old Hickory. Mrs. Wills received a phone call to come immediately to the Canteen House on the railroad level at Union Station. There, she, Mrs. Joseph Howell Jr.; Mrs. I.W. Miller; Nellie Ely Thompson and Miss Kitty Berry worked all day rendering service of every kind. A more pleasant task came that October when the Women's Liberty Loan Committee of the Nashville Chapter American Red Cross arranged a breakfast at the Belle Meade County Club for French Alpine soldiers, who were touring the United States. Mrs. Jessie Wills and fellow members of the ARC Canteen Committee served as waitresses.

While Mamie Craig was attending Annie Allison's School, and cousin Ridley was fast becoming a prominent campus figure at Vanderbilt, Jesse was quietly flourishing in the classroom at Wallace University School on West End across from The Cathedral of the Incarnation. There, he increasingly came under the enormous influence of Professor Clarence B. "Botts" Wallace, a friend of the Willses at First Presbyterian Church and a great educator. At Wallace, boys not only received excellent preparatory school educations but also learned the importance of integrity and character. Although he was slight of build and not an athlete, Jesse endured football and played on the Wallace team as a junior and senior. Although he struggled in athletics, Jesse more than made up by excelling in academics and student government.

Beginning in the summer of 1916, Jesse began working at National Life. He kept up this summer employment until he graduated from Vanderbilt in 1922. As a 17-year-old high school junior in 1916-17, Jesse, who was tall, gangling and shy, was recognized for the sheer brilliance of his mind. According to Geddes Douglas, a schoolmate two years younger, Jesse could read Virgil "in long, sweeping sentences. . . ." As a senior, Jesse's popularity was evident. He was elected vice-chairman of the Honor Committee, editor-in-chief of the *Wallace World*, senior class prophet and Bachelor of Ugliness. One honor he did not win was the presidency of the senior class; that went to Robert McNeilly. Nevertheless, Jesse's academic accomplishments were enough to make his shy younger sister, Mamie Craig, feel that she was walking in a tall shadow.

During their son's junior year at Wallace, Jessie and Ridley considered moving to one of the attractive subdivisions springing up around the Nashville Golf and Country Club seven miles west of town. Smog was a problem on Louise Avenue, and lots of friends had already moved to the clean, fresh air of the country. Consequently, in December 1916, Ridley purchased lots 67 and 68 in the new Golf Club addition at the southwest corner of Westview (then Highland Avenue) and Warner Place.[29] He hoped to build a house there only a long block from the country club, where he was a member of the committee responsible for building the clubhouse and golf course. Closer to Belle Meade Boulevard on Warner Place, Ridley's friend and fellow Haywood County native, Edward I. Webb Jr., already had built a handsome residence designed by Edward Dougherty. Other expensive homes were being built in 1916, both on Warner Place and Harding Place. Although Ridley decided not to build on his Belle Meade lots, he held them as an investment.

At the National Life convention in 1917, ceremonies were held creating the original Old Guard and honoring the 35 field men who had been with the company since 1902, helped it get off the ground and later contributed to its spectacular growth. The company's five early officers – Messrs Craig, Wills, Clements and Tyne, and Dr. Fort – also

---

29   Davidson County Deeds, Book 492, p. 473

were inducted into the Old Guard. Each man received a handsome Old Guard lapel pin featuring 15 pearls, one for each year of service.

In May 1918, Ridley's niece, Harriette Catchings Wills, graduated from high school in Brownsville and married 22-year-old Herbert Exum Oglesby, of Millington. Two years later, Mamie Craig graduated from Annie Allison's School. Following her studies there, Ridley and Jessie Wills, who had always spoiled their only daughter, decided that she might gain more confidence if they sent her to Holton

Harriette Catchings Wills Oglesby (1900–1955)

Arms, a well-respected finishing school in Washington, D. C. for two years of junior college. Jessie and Nell helped Mamie Craig shop for the clothes she would need. Most Nashville girls from socially prominent families shopped at Loveman, Berger and Teitlebaum, which carried the very latest articles of ladies' dress.

At Holton Arms, one of Mamie Craig's classmates was her half first cousin from Atlanta, Margaret Nelson. Mamie Craig graduated from Holton Arms in 1922 with a sufficient appreciation for the school that she sent her daughters, Eleanor and Phoebe, there a generation later. Phoebe, in turn, would influence her first cousin Ellen Wills to attend Holton. Much later, Ellen served on the Holton Arms Board of Trustees.[30]

The biggest business challenges facing Mr. Craig, Mr. Clements and Mr. Wills at National Life in 1919 was the fact that, by limiting the company to the field of industrial health and accident insurance, the earnings opportunities of their field men were limited by the lack of other types of policies to sell. Their decision to go into the field of

---

30   For decades, Ellen Wills Martin has been an active communicant at Christ Episcopal Church in Georgetown. For many of those years, her rector was the Rev. Sanford Garner Jr., D.C., a native of Henning, Tennessee and a descendant of the Mann family. Ellen has always appreciated their distant kinship.

58

life insurance with an Ordinary Department was akin to starting a new company. To head the new operation, they chose Edwin W. Craig, the son of C.A. Craig. His assistant would be Eldon Stevenson Jr. These two young men, both Vanderbilt graduates and close friends, had experienced a wide range of company operations since they started with the company in 1913. Entering the life insurance business meant that the company would need its own actuary. W.H. McBride was employed, which relieved Ridley Wills of his duties as unofficial actuary. The company's entry into the life insurance business also meant that a full time medical director was needed. Dr. Fort disposed of his infirmary and his private practice and came into the home office on a full-time basis.

The Ordinary Department initially issued three plans of insurance – whole life, 20-payment life, and 20-year endowment. The ordinary production steadily increased and by the end of five years had reached $40 million of life insurance in force.

The idea of building an appropriate memorial to honor those Tennesseans who had given their lives in the World War surfaced in 1919. After considering a number of locations, including Centennial Park, the Tennessee State Legislature passed a bill authorizing the purchase of all property located in an area bounded by Sixth and Seventh avenues and Union and Cedar streets. This included the governor's mansion, the Masonic Grand Lodge, a large number of elegant homes, and National Life's home office. The company would have to move. Three senior officers, C.A. Craig, Ridley Wills, and Tom Tyne were named to a committee to identify an appropriate site. One possibility was the Nashville YMCA building across Union Street. The YMCA was having financial difficulties and might be willing to sell. The committee met with YMCA President Horace G. Hill, who was not interested and who provided financial muscle and leadership that enabled the YMCA to rally and keep their handsome building. The National Life executives then focused their attention on homes owned by the J. Horton Fall and Robert G. Thorne families at 303 and 305 Union Street. They successfully purchased these properties, and a building committee, consisting of Mr. Clements, Dr. Fort and Mr. Tyne was appointed. Construction on a handsome five-story office building began in July 1922 and was completed late in 1923. Ridley Wills described the 60,000-square-foot building to the sales force as "The South's most beautiful home."

At the dedication, held February 19, 1924, 600 people, including 250 field men, were present. The only note of sadness was the absence of "the beloved Ridley Wills, vice-president and close pioneer associate of President C.A. Craig, whose health keeps him in the west and far from a scene to whose happy coming he had contributed so much." [31] When Ridley was able to return to work after being in a sanitarium on this or some other occasion in the mid to late 1920s, National life employees erected a huge welcome sign nine feet high at the front entrance of the home office building. Each letter was composed of the words, "Welcome Home, Mr. Wills."

Another historic event came on the evening of October 5, 1924, when National Life began broadcasting on the company's new radio station – WSM. Edwin Craig, who had a passion for radio, had been interested in starting the station for several years and finally talked his father, Mr. Wills, Mr. Clements, Dr. Fort and Mr. Tyne into giving the station a chance. Mr. Wills admitted that Edwin faced serious resistance from the board "but kept hammering away for some three years" and finally convinced them to give him the go-ahead. Edwin's argument was that the station would cement the company's identity in its listening area, be good public relations, benefit the community and support the company's field men with prospects and policyholders. WSM, which stands for "We Shield Millions," began as a 1,000-watt station, one of only two in the entire South. Edwin was right. Later, Mr. Wills said, "thanks to WSM, the name of National is now on the very air we breathe." The

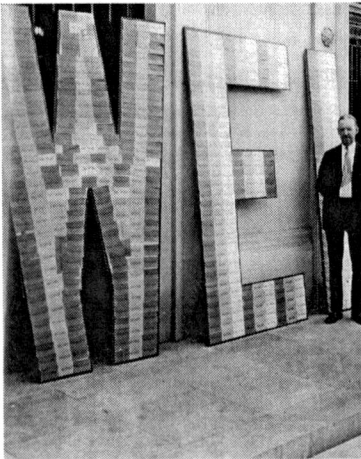

Ridley Wills standing beside the "Welcome Home Mr. Wills" sign erected on the front steps of the National Life and Accident Insurance Company home office, 1924.

---

31   "Dedicate New Life Building," *Nashville Banner*, February 21, 1924.

National Life Home Office Building

studio and control room were on the fifth floor of the new building, and Edwin was given responsibility for overseeing the operation. Not long after the station went on the air, George D. Hay, of WLS in Chicago, was named director. Under his leadership, country music performers Uncle Jimmy Thompson and Dr. Humphrey Bate's "Possum Hunters" made their debuts and began performing on what was called the "WSM Barn Dance" every Saturday night. One day Hay spontaneously coined the phrase "Grand Ole Opry." The country music show was an immediate success and, when the five-story wing was added along Union Street in 1929, WSM expanded its studio on the fifth floor by adding additional space for spectators, who were separated from the show by a glass partition. WSM's first singing star was the fabulous Uncle Dave Macon, the Dixie Dewdrop. His famous line was "When my baby walks down the street, all the little birdies go peep peep peep."

In October 1925, WSM began broadcasting the Sunday evening worship services of Nashville's First Presbyterian Church. Made possible through the influence of elder Ridley Wills, this was the first radio broadcast of a church service in the South. A church bulletin that month stated, "Beginning next Sunday night, the Sunday evening sermons and services in this church will be sent out on radio through the courtesy of the National Life and Accident Insurance Company. Their new station, WSM, has been graciously put at the discretion of First Presbyterian Church for this purpose. It is a big contribution toward the proclamation of the gospel. The First Church is deeply grateful to the National Life for this substantial evidence of the company's interest in the things that make for right living in our country." Soon, radio sets, consisting of a receiver box and a set of earphones, were delivered to all the congregation's shut-ins, as well as to the Old Woman's Home on West End Avenue.

CHAPTER VI

The fall of 1918 brought two big changes to Jesse's life. He joined the army and entered Vanderbilt University, where three generations of Wills men, Ridley, Jesse and Jesse's son, Ridley II, would all serve on the Board of Trust. Technically, Jesse joined the Student Army Training Corps. To do so he had to pass an eye examination. Because he had only 10 percent vision in one eye, he successfully memorized the eye chart. When Jesse enlisted at 19, he had brown eyes, a fair complexion, and dark hair. He stood slightly over six feet in height and probably weighed something in the neighborhood of 140 pounds. Jesse served only three months in the S.A.T.C. because World War I ended that November.

At Vanderbilt, where Jesse majored in English, a number of his professors remembered his first cousin Ridley as being different and very bright. The Head of the English Department was Professor Eddie Mims. Three other outstanding English professors under whom Jesse studied were John Crowe Ransom, Walter Clyde Curry and Donald Davidson. Soon, Davidson and Wills became close friends. As a freshman, Jesse wrote a theme for Davidson contrasting *Grimm's Fairy Tales* unfavorably with the Oz books written by L. Frank Baum. Davidson liked the theme so much he read the paper to the class.

In college, Jesse built upon the classical background he received at Wallace. His favorite subjects were English and history; geology was the only science he really enjoyed. During his freshman and sophomore years, he was a member of the Blue Pencil Club. In his junior year, he joined the Calumet Club, the most prestigious literary club on campus. There he won the praise of his close friend and brilliant classmate, Allen Tate. Jesse, Allen and some other members of the Calumet Club had become involved with another literary group, which, although it was not officially a part of Vanderbilt, was creating a great deal of excitement on campus. This group was the now famous Fugitive poets who still bring prestige to Nashville and Vanderbilt. It had its genesis in March 1922 when Sidney Hirsch and James Frank, brothers-in-law, sat in the library of Frank's home on Whitland Avenue, where they decided that then was a good time for young Nashville poets to publish a literary magazine. A month later, a Nashville newspaper reported, "The Fugitive, a new local periodical devoted to poetry, is to make its bow to the public in the next few days when the first issue will be off the press. The literary talent of Nashville boasts a group of young poets, both of the Vanderbilt community and of the city, who possess marked poetic talent and whose work has appeared in leading magazines. This group of eight or ten will compose an informal editorial board, the usual editor-in-chief and a formal staff being omitted by these talented conferees. The poems are to be published over pen names, thus adding a spice of mystery to the interest of the periodical. From three to five numbers will be issued annually."

In his senior year, Jesse was president of Phi Delta Theta Fraternity, possibly the strongest fraternity on campus. In those days, there was no drinking in fraternity houses, but there was plenty of moonshine elsewhere, and the Phis were not reluctant about indulging. Jesse was, however, moderate in his drinking habits – as in everything else.

In September 1922, four months after Jesse graduated, his first cousin Ridley Wills II (son of Mann and Della) returned to Vanderbilt from New York, where he had been a reporter for a large newspaper and where he had written a novel, *Hoax*, published by Doran and Company. That fall, Ridley roomed with Robert Penn Warren, a much younger English major. The following March, Allen Tate returned to Vanderbilt, after having dropped out for a year due to illness. Soon, the three young men were rooming together at Wesley Hall. Louise Cowan later wrote, "It was a wild and boisterous time for all three, when they were intellectually snobbish, no doubt full of pretense and pose, yet withal, intensely vulnerable to poetry, and for all their sophistication,

William Ridley Wills II, at age 23 (1897–1957)

innocent of the ways of the world."[32] One evening, in the spring of 1923, Ridley and Allen walked down to a pie wagon and wrote the entire *The Golden Mean and Other Poems.* The purpose of the work was threefold: First, to parody Professor Edwin Mims and his theory of the balance between modernism and traditionalism. Second, the *Golden Mean* was an attempt to poke fun at the high seriousness that attended the Fugitive meetings and dominated the *Fugitive Magazine.* Thirdly, in one instance, Tate and Wills used the small production as a means of satirizing T.S. Eliot's *The Waste Land,* published in 1922. Tate had earlier been so taken with *The Waste Land* that he illustrated the walls of their room at Wesley Hall with scenes from the work.

To publicize *The Golden Mean and Other Poems,* Ridley nailed fliers on telephone poles around Nashville. People who read the flyers had never heard of Ridley and assumed his well-known uncle, Ridley Wills had written the poem. Part of this time, Mr. Wills was at City View Sanitarium on Murfreesboro Pike, where he was recuperating from a spell of depression. Still, he and Jessie heard about what his nephew was up to. They also were embarrassed that Ridley was writing bad checks. Once, Ridley borrowed some money from his father to pay Allen Tate's tuition at Vanderbilt, or, at least, that is what he told his father.

Quickly, the *Fugitive Magazine* drew the attention of the literary world. In July, H.L. Mencken, super critic and arch detractor of the South, wrote in the *Baltimore Sun* that the *Fugitive Magazine* was Tennessee's one and only literary production. Mencken said he was recommending the magazine to the attention of other critics. Surprisingly, Chancellor Kirkland and Eddie Mims were anything but enthusiastic.

Jesse joined the Fugitive group sometime before April 12, 1923, when the members included:

> Dr. Walter Clyde Curry, Vanderbilt faculty
> Donald Davidson, Vanderbilt faculty
> James M. Frank, Nashville businessman
> Sidney Hirsch, playwright
> Stanley Johnson, Vanderbilt faculty
> Merrill Moore, Vanderbilt student

---

32   Louise Cowan, *The Fugitive Group*

John Crowe Ransom, Vanderbilt faculty
Alex B. Stevenson, Nashville businessman
Allen Tate, former Vanderbilt student
Jesse Wills, Vanderbilt graduate
Ridley Wills II, Vanderbilt student

Ridley Wills II graduated from Vanderbilt in 1923 with a B.A. degree. *The Commodore* cited him as the author of *"The Hoax,"* and joint perpetrator of *"The Golden Mean."* It said he also wrote a daily column titled "Random Talk with Ridley Wills" and was a member of Sigma Upsilon Literary Society, *The Hustler* staff (1923) and The Calumet Club (1923). With many of its contributors having left Nashville, the Fugitive group, after publishing a total of 19 issues of *Fugitive Magazine*, decided to discontinue publication in December 1925.

While Jesse was in Vanderbilt and Mamie Craig at Holton Arms, Mr. Wills was on an emotional roller coaster. He experienced frightening periods of depression followed by abnormal highs. With adequate treatment unavailable in Nashville, Ridley sought relief at sanitariums across the country. Often, Jesse accompanied him. There must have been a period of stability in 1922, however, as that year Wills was elected a Ruling Elder of the First Presbyterian Church. Two years earlier, he was elected treasurer of Nashville's Protestant Hospital. Possibly, his own health problems may have led him to become involved in establishing that health facility.

The allure of the western and southern suburbs was quite strong in the 1920s. By 1924, Edwin and Elizabeth Craig had moved to their new home in Belle Meade Park.[33] Soon, the C. Runcie Clements and the

---

33   The Edwin Craigs bought a lot and built a two-story, stucco home at 4433 Shepard Place. They had not lived on State Street, however, since 1917, when they moved to Apt. A-2 in the Dunraven Apartments at the corner of 23rd Avenue North and Elliston Place. In 1933, the Craigs moved to a house at 540 Belle Meade Blvd. that had been built in 1926-27 by F. J. McCarthy. The house, one of Nashville's first fireproof residences, was designed by Asmus and Clark.

Neely Craigs also moved to Belle Meade.[34] Despite this, Ridley and Jessie Wills hesitated, possibly because of his health. In July 1925, he sold his lots in Belle Meade to Robert "Bob" Rives for $2,075.[35] With the help of her parents, Eleanor and Bob Rives built a small, clapboard cottage on the property at 4401 Warner Place.

After Jesse graduated from Vanderbilt in June 1922, he went to work for National Life. People often asked him if he ever considered teaching. Jesse said, "Teaching was no temptation. I didn't see much future to it. In fact, teaching seemed a little bit futile. I wasn't excited about going into business either. But my father was ill. I felt duty-bound to go into the business he had helped found."

Professor Mims tried to talk Jesse into making teaching his career. Years later, Jesse wrote Allen Tate about his decision to go into the insurance business. He said that, although he knew he had some ability to write, he felt he really had no alternative. He lacked self-confidence and had several personal problems all related to his father's bad health. "I had to spend a great part of my time as companion to him and had to go off on several long trips with him to such places as Battle Creek and Johns Hopkins and similar sanitariums. This happened just as I was starting in adult life."[36]

When Mamie Craig returned to Nashville after graduating from Holton Arms, she became active in the younger social set by joining the Girls' Cotillion Club and the Junior League of Nashville. She and Jesse continued to live with their parents on Louise. Their telephone must have been kept busy, as Mamie Craig and her friends discussed young men and other matters of interest.

---

34   The C. Runcie Clements built "Waters Meet," a lovely home overlooking Richland Creek at 116 Jackson Blvd. Meanwhile, the C.A. Craigs moved in 1924 to a large Colonial residence at 504 Belle Meade Blvd. that had been designed by Hart, Freeland and Roberts for M.A. Dabney. Until then they had been living at 2214 State St., having moved there from next door after their son, Edwin, and his wife, Elizabeth, moved to the Dunraven Apartments in 1918. Professor Clarence B. Wallace and his family lived in the home at 2214 State St. after the C.A. Craigs moved to Belle Meade.

35   copy of Indenture, dated July 1925

36   Jesse Wills wrote two sonnets entitled "Fear," which dealt with his father's first mental illness, which was both profound and seemingly causeless. The sonnets appear in his book, *Early and Late*.

Despite the telephone, life on Louise Avenue quieted somewhat for the Wills family in the 1920s. Mr. Wills continued to pour his energies into National Life, while Jessie involved herself with a number of traditional activities, including luncheons and teas at the Centennial Club.[37] However, there were exceptions, such as the night in 1922 when a number of the neighbors heard Runcie Clements, normally a very mild-mannered gentleman, chew out his daughter Julia's date. Julia, then 15-years-old, and a girlfriend of hers went on a double date with two 16-year-old boys who had just begun driving. When the boys brought the apple of Runcie's eye home much later than they should have, he was hopping mad. As the young man escorted Julia to the front steps, Clements opened the front door and accosted him for having Julia out so late. He continued to berate him all the way to the car. The other boy, Guilford Dudley Jr., slumped down in the seat to escape Clements' unexpected wrath.

In 1928, Julia would marry former Vanderbilt baseball star G. Dan Brooks, a young man who, during his playing days at Vandy, had been befriended by Mr. Wills. In time, he went to work at National Life, ultimately succeeding Jesse Wills as chairman of the board in 1968. Brooks carried an enormous respect for Mr. Wills personally, and for his uncanny ability with figures. In 1980, Brooks recalled, "Ridley Wills had the most brilliant mind of any man I have ever known. He could remember figures related to the company 20 years before. He wasn't an athlete, but he used to walk to see the baseball practices at Vanderbilt, where I was a player, and it was there where we first got acquainted. Later, I stopped by his house several times to play horseshoes with him."[38]

In September 1924, Mann and Della's daughter, Elizabeth, entered Vanderbilt as a junior, having transferred from George Peabody College. Before attending Peabody she had spent one year at Gulf Park Junior College. At Vanderbilt, Elizabeth was a member of Delta Delta Delta Sorority, the Bachelor Maids in 1924-25 (the most representative girls in the junior and senior classes), and president of the *Scribblers* her senior

---

37   In 1937, Mrs. Ridley Wills was elected a director of the Centennial Club.

38   Conversation, G. Daniel Brooks with Alan Costa, March 31, 1980.

year. Ridley was proud of his niece, and he and Jessie enjoyed having her at their home for dinner on several occasions.

When Elizabeth graduated in 1926, with a major in English, she had her sights on teaching high school or college English. Thinking she could get a better job if she had a master's degree, she entered Columbia University that fall, where she got her master's in teaching. Once, while in New York City, she got a long-distance phone call from Allen Tate that struck her as unusual – he wanted her to read a poem he'd written the next time she was in Nashville. Elizabeth told him she would be happy to do so and sometime later met Allen in the lobby of the Hermitage Hotel. After greeting each other, Allen handed her the poem and asked Elizabeth to read it and give him her opinion. She said, "Allen, I'll read it tonight and get back with you tomorrow morning." Allen said, "No, I want you to read it now." She agreed to do so and sat down in the lobby to study the poem. In a few minutes, Allen said, "What do you think?" Elizabeth, never one to mince words, said, "Allen, it doesn't make any sense." Allen never again consulted Elizabeth about his poetry. She went on to an outstanding career as a superlative English teacher for 40 years at Haywood County High School, Whitehaven, Tenn. High School and Memphis East High School. She also did graduate work at Peabody College and Memphis State.

During the early 1920s, Elizabeth corresponded regularly with Vachel Lindsay, who had been the poet in residence during her year at Gulf Park Junior College. He fell in love with Elizabeth and visited her in Brownsville. At some point, Vachel gave her an engagement ring. She declined, having no interest in marrying a man 23 years her senior. They continued to correspond, however, and he dedicated several of his poems to her. In May 1925, Lindsay married Elizabeth Connor, who bore him two children. Depressed over financial problems and worn out from a six-month road trip, he committed suicide in 1931. Elizabeth also was a good friend of writer Eleanor Ruggles, the author of *The West-Going Heart: A Life of Vachel Lindsay*. One of the characters in Ruggles' book was based on Elizabeth.[39]

Death struck the National Life founding family first in July 1925 when

---

39   Letter, Elizabeth Wills to Jesse E. Wills, January 12, 1977, collection of the author.

E.B. Craig, vice president and manager of the Investment Department, and a member of the board of trust since 1903, died after an illness of several weeks. Ridley wrote about his mentor's death in the company's employee magazine, saying: "He was the gentlest, the kindliest of men, He loved his fellows and was by them beloved. He lived a life of integrity and there was never a spot on the record he made." At Craig's funeral, Ridley's mind must have wandered to that December evening in Bristol when E.B. encouraged Neely and him to make a play for the National Sick and Accident Association.

During the 1920s, Ridley Wills continued to take a keen interest in neighborhood children, as well as his nieces and nephew and the children of National Life employees. George McIntosh, son of a longtime National Life employee, remembered that Wills gave him a shiny, new quarter each Christmas. Henriette Weaver Jackson, whose cousins, Martha and Mary Williamson, grew up on Louise Avenue during the 1920s, recalled in 1993 that Wills would come out when she and her cousins were playing or skating on the sidewalk and offer them sticks of King Leo Peppermint candy from a round tin.[40] Julia Clements and her next-door neighbor and best friend, Ann McLemore, were often in the Wills house.[41] Willie Geny and other neighborhood boys frequently played marbles on both State Street and Louise Avenue. Occasionally, Wills and Craig would be talking on the sidewalk nearby. Once, Willie said Wills gave him an agate and asked him and his friends if they would mind resuming their game a little further down the street.[42]

---

40   In 1923, Mary and Martha Williamson moved with their widowed mother, Mary Ready Weaver Williamson, to an apartment at 207 Louise Ave. Their landlady was Mrs. H.F. Kirkpatrick, who shared the duplex with the Williamsons.

41   Ann was the daughter of John B. and Annie McLemore. Although trained as a lawyer, McLemore was secretary and manager of the Overland Grain Company. He and his family moved to 2216 State St. in about 1919 after the C.A. Craigs moved from that address to the house next door (2214) where the Edwin Craigs had lived until their move to the Dunraven Apartments in 1918. In 1923, the McLemores moved to Johnson City, Tennessee. Nine years later, their daughter Ann married Coleman Harwell.

42   In the 1920s and for several decades after that, one of Nashville's larger oak trees grew in the middle of the 200 block of Louise Avenue. Rather than destroy the tree, the city simply paved the street on either side of the tree.

CHAPTER VII

Ridley and Jessie were thrilled that, after Jesse's graduation from Vanderbilt, he decided to come to work at National Life. Jesse's first assignment was a clerical position in the Agents Records Division of the Ordinary Department. He soon became somewhat bored with the routine job, which did not fit well with his artistic temperament. In 1924, he was promoted to be Eldon Stevenson's assistant. This qualified him for a secretary. At that time, he was dating one of the girls in the Ordinary Department, Louise Hill, a beautiful blonde. Louise was fond of Jesse but also was dating two other men at the same time, the handsome Walker Casey, and C.R. "Tot" McCullough, a starting tackle on the 1922 Vanderbilt football team. Louise suggested to Jesse that he ask another young woman and co-employee, Louise Willett, to be his secretary. Louise Willett and Louise Hill were closest friends from the same hometown of Adams, Tennessee. Louise Willett liked the idea, and Stevenson promoted her to be Jesse's secretary. Soon, Louise Hill left the company to marry McCullough.

Louise Willett was a pretty girl with brown eyes and a nice smile. Always cheerful and carefree, she often hummed a song and enjoyed watering the flowers on the windowsill of the office. She did not know that her lively personality reminded Jesse of spring and that she was the inspiration for his poem "Primavera." After a time, Louise left the company to marry Joseph Puryear, a young Nashville businessman. Years later, Louise remembered Jesse Wills as "a precious, intelligent man who had a keen sense of humor. I don't believe he ever had an enemy," she recalled. Louise also was fond of Jesse's father. Many times, when Jesse had late meetings, Mr. Wills would drive her to her home at the corner of 21st and Murphy avenues, four blocks from his house on Louise.

Jesse, who had inherited a gift for control of figures and matters of detail from his father, moved up quickly in National Life's management team. He was named manager of the Agents Records Division in 1925, and a member of the board of directors the next year. During the decade, he was invited to join the Old Oak Club, a prestigious literary club that had been founded in 1888. For the rest of his life, Jesse would be a member of that club, which stimulated his interest in writing.[43] He also wrote book reviews for *The Nashville Tennessean* during his early days at National Life.

By 1924, the Wills' daughter, Mamie Craig, had fallen in love with Clinton Pennington "Ted" Clark, a personable World War I veteran who was helping his widowed mother, Phebe Eastgate Clark, run the Tennessee, Kentucky and Northern Railroad, a short-line railroad that ran from Algood, near Cookeville, to Livingston, Tennessee. Mrs. Clark's husband, George Clark, a veteran railroad executive with the Illinois Central and the Tennessee Central, had bought the line a few years before his death in 1914. Their only child, Ted, who was born February 2, 1899, had received his education at Nashville's Montgomery Bell Academy and at the University of Cincinnati, where he was a member of Delta Tau Delta fraternity. During the First World War, he served with the 34th Division of Engineers in France. One of his prized possessions was a German helmet he brought home.

Ted and Mamie Craig's wedding was scheduled for June 1, 1925. Mrs. Wills decided that it would be an informal affair at home at 6:30 on a Monday evening.[44] Dr. Albert C.

Ridley Wills persuing a "Book of Remembrances" presented to him on Christmas 1925 from "Shield Men" everywhere.

Holt, the assistant minister at First Presbyterian, officiated. The petite,

---

43   Jesse also was a member of the Coffee House Club from 1953 until his death in 1977.

44   It is puzzling why Mrs. Wills chose to have an informal wedding for Mamie Craig on a Monday night. Normally, one would think a life insurance official as prominent as Mr. Wills, would have a large church wedding for his only daughter. It seems likely that Mr. Wills' health was a factor. This is strengthened by the fact that Mamie Craig's brother, Jesse, not her father, escorted her down the stairway to the altar in the living room.

blonde bride stood five feet, two inches tall and probably weighed no more than 105 pounds. She came down the stairway escorted by her brother, Jesse. At the altar in the living room they were met by Mr. Wills, who gave his daughter away, and the groom, who was slender, dark-haired and handsome. The bridesmaids were Mamie Craig's cousins from Atlanta, Misses Margaret and Louise Nelson. Ted's best man was Paul Stumb, son of the co-owner of Stumb's Drug Store on Fourth Avenue North. After the wedding, Jessie and Ridley gave a reception and buffet supper in their home that was decorated with ferns, palms and large clusters of lilies. A quartet provided music for the wedding and reception attended by family members and intimate friends. Out-of-town guests included Charlotte and Henry Nelson of Atlanta, who brought their daughters, Mary, Margaret and Louise, to be bridesmaids. Mrs. Nelson was Mrs. Wills' half-sister. Mamie Craig's uncle and aunt, Mann and Della Wills, of Brownsville, came, and so did Agnes Lipscomb Whiteside, the 82-year-old wife of Mamie Craig's great uncle, Henry C. Whiteside, from Shelbyville.

After the wedding, Mamie Craig and Ted went on a six-week-long wedding trip out West, where they visited the Grand Canyon, Yellowstone Park, San Francisco and Los Angeles. Upon their return, they moved to Livingston, Tennessee, where they built a house and where Mamie Craig rode with Ted in his steam engine from Algood to Livingston. Mamie Craig was unhappy in such an unsophisticated town, and by 1926 was back in Nashville where Ted opened an office in the Independent Life Building. In the Nashville City Directory for 1926, he was listed as vice-president of the Tennessee, Kentucky and Northern Railroad. Mamie Craig set up housekeeping in No. 6 in the Halcyon Apartments at 3800 Harding Road. She was thrilled to be reunited with such friends as Dot Tucker Coleman and Van Meter Blackie. In 1927, Ted started his own advertising business, C.P. Clark Inc., although he retained his title as vice-president of his mother's railroad through the balance of the decade. Two years later, he and Mamie Craig moved to a house at 220 Craighead Ave. that Mr. Wills bought for them. In 1930, Ted accepted a position as vice president for advertising for General Shoe Corporation. There a young man, Charles Coggin, would work for Clark. Coggin told Ridley Wills II in the 1990s that Ted Clark was the best advertising man he ever saw – a creative genius. In the 1930s, he would be elected to the board of Montgomery Bell Academy. In addition to enjoying the advertising business, Ted loved trains, airplanes and boats.

Ridley and Jessie's happiness over Mamie Craig's marriage was tempered by his periodic periods of depression and by the death on August 8, 1927, of Jessie's sister, Nellie Ely Thompson, who left a husband, T. Leigh Thompson, but no children. Their only child, an infant daughter born July 7, 1905, had died at birth.

Although Ridley missed the dedication of the new home office building in 1924 due to his illness, he was on hand when the company celebrated its Silver anniversary in 1926. On that occasion, the progress of the company was heralded and the field force recognized for their efforts in propelling the company forward. The growth of assets from $19,967.32 at the close of 1901 to $15,276,325.15 at the end of 1925 revealed the tremendous growth of the insurance company.

During the late 1920s, Ridley probably attended the annual Taylor family reunion at Tabernacle United Methodist Church. This Brownsville tradition began in the summer of 1826 when the Taylor family first gathered at Tabernacle to hear preaching, see their relatives and eat fried chicken and other good Southern food. From then until well into the 21st century, generations of Taylors from all over the country converged on the campground each August or early September to enjoy themselves and reestablish family links.[45] The Taylor family used cloth tents in the early years and later built small log cabins. Eventually, they would build much larger cabins. Grandma Tamar Taylor, Polk Taylor's widow and the African-American family matriarch, had cooked at Tabernacle United Methodist Church since 1922.

In the 1920s and 1930s, Mann and Della Wills and their children and grandchildren were frequent attendees.[46] Their granddaughter, Virginia Sturdivant, camped out at Tabernacle every summer with her parents, Bob and Trousdale Sturdivant, from the time she was eight-months-old

---

45 Deceased Taylor family members had been laid to rest at Tabernacle Cemetery since 1829.

46 In 1881, Ruth Taylor married Nicholas Perkins Thornton. They became the parents of seven sons – Richard, Macon, John, Marion, Harbert, Nick and Robert – and a single daughter, Ruth.

until she was about ten.

Mann Wills also spent time in the 1920s with his grandsons. He taught Robert Wills Sturdivant, Virginia's brother, and the Mann's oldest grandson, how to hunt, fish and camp. Bob would retain a love for the outdoor life as long as he lived.[47] Bob's first cousins, Herbert Wills Oglesby and Mann Wills Oglesby remembered going to Tabernacle every August, driving with their grandfather to Sunkist Beach, swimming in Wills Creek at the end of Park Avenue and going to Mr. Wills' famed Sunday School Class.[48] One thing that Mann Wills did not do very often was to go to Memphis. When he went in 1928 to attend a Broadway of America Highway meeting,[49] it was his first visit since 1892.

In the spring of 1929, Ridley Wills gave the commencement address at Haywood County High School. Later that day, while driving around the public square, Ridley noticed young Clarence Berson, who had received his diploma that morning, sitting on the courthouse steps. Wills stopped and asked Clarence, whose parents, Clarence and Louise Berson, were friends of his, where he was going to college. Clarence said he guessed he would go to Southwestern College in Memphis. Wills suggested that, instead, he come to Nashville and attend Vanderbilt. Wills offered to help by giving Clarence a part-time job at National Life. Clarence took his advice and entered Vanderbilt, where he played end on the football team in 1931, 1932 and 1933 and worked part-time at National Life. After graduation from Vanderbilt, Clarence went on to spend his entire business career at National Life, working with three generations of the Wills family – Ridley Wills; his son, Jesse Wills; and Jesse's son, Ridley Wills II. At his retirement in 1977, Berson was a senior vice-president of National Life and chairman of NLT Computer Services.

Rose Mary Mann was another young person from Brownsville

---

47   The author's first cousin, George Wills Crook, was named for his grandfather, George Clark. After Mamie Craig divorced Ted Clark and married Senter Crook, George's name was legally changed from Clark to Crook.

48   David Womack Wills wrote, in his book, *Depression Daze*, that Wills Creek was named for his great-uncle Ridley Wills.

49   U.S. Highway 70 originally ran from coast to coast, beginning in eastern North Carolina and ending in California near the Pacific Coast. Because it was one of the main east-west thoroughfares in America, it was called the "Broadway of America." In Tennessee, U.S. 70 connected Knoxville, Nashville and Memphis, and ran through Brownsville.

whom Ridley helped. After she graduated from West Tennessee Business College, Wills was instrumental in getting her a job as a secretary at National Life.

From the beginning of National Life, company stock had been closely held by the founders and their family members. By the late1920s, when National Life's assets had grown so spectacularly, friends and investors clamored for some of the stock. In response to this local demand, Richard Shillinglaw, vice president of the securities subsidiary of the American National Bank, approached the senior National Life executives with a proposal that they each sell 25 percent of their stock. His presentation must have been convincing. On December 28, 1928, each National Life stockholder put a quarter of his or her stock in a pool. Soon, 6,250 shares were delivered to the American National Company. The stock initially went on the market at $880 a share. It was so heavily oversubscribed that within 10 days, the stock advanced to $925 bid. By September 29, 1929, the price was quoted at $1,120 bid and $1,145 asked. On October 14, the market crashed, leading to the Great Depression. In this environment, there was little activity in the stock. By year's end, the price quoted was $950 bid, $1,000 asked with little or none changing hands. This initial public offering would make it possible for Ridley to do things that otherwise would have been impossible.

Having substantial liquid assets for the first time in his life, Ridley Wills thought first about his family. On October 23, 1929, he set up a trust with the Bank of New York and Trust Company, 48 Wall St., New York, New York, to benefit Jessie, who would get one-half the income during her lifetime, and his two children, each of whom would get one-fourth of the income during their lifetimes. At the deaths of Jesse and Mamie Craig, the income would go to their children, per stirpes, for a period of 21 years thereafter. In 1932, after Matt Buckner Wills was born, the trust was amended to provide for the termination of Jesse's part to 21 years after the death of Matt, in the event he survived his father. Other changes would be made as other grandchildren were born.

Ridley also increased his benevolences. Among his favorite charities were the First Presbyterian Church, the Community Chest, Fisk and Vanderbilt universities, the YMCA Graduate School, the American Red Cross, the Girls Christian home and Monroe Harding Children's Home, where he was a trustee.[50]

With plenty of money in their pockets for the first time, the founders of National Life could afford to build new homes, primarily in the city's exclusive, new residential neighborhood anchored by the new Nashville Golf and Country Club and Mr. Percy Warner's streetcar line that had been extended from Wilson's Switch to the new club in what was called The Highlands of Belle Meade. The Wills surprised their friends by deciding to build their new home not in Belle Meade but on land off the Franklin Road that had been owned in 1887 by Van Leer Kirkman and sold by him to Col. John Overton. On September 9, 1929, Attorney J.M. Peebles, of Tyne, Peebles, Henry & Tyne handed W.R. Wills a deed from Emma W. Cain and husband to Wills and his wife, Jessie, for 10,436 acres of land in the 7th Civil District of Davidson County. He said, "This deed vests a fee simple title in you and Mrs. Wills. The consideration was $18,263. "This consideration is arrived at on the basis of $1,750 per acre for 10,463 acres." Because the former conveyance from H.C. and Beulah B. Weber to Emma W. Cain specified that the property contained 10.54 acres, Mr. Wills suggested that they split the difference of $182 and he pay Mrs. Cain $18,354. She agreed, and the land transaction was completed. Ridley and Jessie also bought a smaller parcel from Gideon Wade. Later, the Wills gave this lot to their daughter, Mamie Craig. There, in 1940 and 1941, Mamie Craig and her husband, Ted Clark, would build the house that Henry and Sarah Cannon later owned. Mamie Craig and Ted had three children, Eleanor, born in 1930, Phoebe, born in 1933, and George born in 1937.

Mr. C.A. Craig and Mr. Mac Peebles, National Life's general counsel, both talked to Wills in 1929 and several times in the 1930s, over the possibility of him writing his last will and testament. Despite Peebles urging him to do so, Wills resisted the idea, telling Peebles that he was satisfied for the state to divide his assets at his death between his wife and two children. Wills never changed his mind on this important issue.

---

50   When Ridley Wills II returned from the field to the National Life home office in 1962, he met a longtime employee who had grown up at Monroe Harding Children's home. The man said that after his graduation from high school, Ridley Wills had given him a job at National Life. He told Ridley II that Mr. Wills gave jobs to a number of Monroe Harding graduates.

Ridley Wills was in a euphoric mood in 1929. National Life had gone public a year before, bringing him wealth for the first time in his life. He also had seemingly recovered from a long but intermittent period of depression that had started when his son, Jesse, was at Vanderbilt. It was during this period of well-being that he decided to build his wife the house of her dreams. Jessie, who had expensive tastes, may have been influenced to want a large home by her friends, Mabel and Leslie Cheek, who built Cheekwood in 1929, and by Jane and Tom Tyne, who would begin construction of their elegant home, Longleat, on Hillsboro Pike in 1929. For the Wills to build a home with six master-size bedrooms, each with a private bath, made little sense to their daughter, Mamie Craig, who had married Ted Clark in 1925 and was living elsewhere. Although their 29-year-old son, Jesse, was living with them, Mr. and Mrs. Wills knew he was seriously courting Ellen Buckner and would likely marry and move to an apartment or house of his own in the not-too-distant future.

Jesse described the construction of Far Hills, in 1971, when he wrote:

"Dad engaged the firm of Hart Freeland & Roberts to design the house and gave Russell Hart, who was the architect of the three, an absolutefree hand in its design. Mr. Roberts and Mr. Freeland were engineers. Mr. Roberts had the main responsibility of seeing that Mr. Hart's artistic ideaswere carried out properly. There has been confusion about the style of the house. To Mr. Hart the house was purely Georgian. It should be remembered that this English architectural style took some of its inspiration from Italy. Mr. W. F. Holt was the contractor. Construction was started in the fall of 1929, and Mr. and Mrs. Wills moved in during the summer of 1931 though the house was not completely finished. I think I was responsible for giving it the name 'Far Hills' because of the view of distant hills from the front terrace. The house was a splendid edifice far beyond the needs of one couple. Mr. Wills' daughter had been married for some years, and I, his son, had married in June 1930. He took great pleasure in it, however. It was characteristic of him that he gave a barbecue party on the place for all the men who had worked on it shortly after he and Jessie moved there.

The house cost more than $150,000, not counting the price of the land. It is hard for me to estimate how much it would cost now. It was splendidly built of the very best material, and functionally embodied all the latest ideas of the time. Mr. Hart also handled the decorations and furnishings with the help of his wife. My mother, naturally, was mostly responsible for decisions in this field. The draperies were very handsome and some of the carpets were especially woven in Austria. A Chippendale table and chairs were ordered for the dining room, and other Georgian reproductions procured for the library. A fine suite of French furniture went into the guest bedroom. There were several extra bedrooms upstairs, however.

My mother, because of memories of her youth in Shelbyville and Nashville, was very fond of Victorian furniture and a fine set of elaborately carved Belter furniture went into the drawing room. By the way, the room that steps down from this was called the Sun Room. The walls were of unfinished brick, and the comfortable furniture was wicker. For years innher bedroom, Mother had a huge Mahogany four-poster bed, and there was another smaller tester bed of maple in another bedroom. Both these pieces were old.

I have failed to mention the grounds. Hart Freeland & Roberts secured as a landscape architect a gentleman who was employed in that capacity at Peabody College. Unfortunately, I cannot recall his name. He died suddenly a very few years later. He did a splendid job for the mansion. There was a reflecting pool behind the house that, of course, still exists. Between it and the garage drive were first a long narrow rock garden and a lovely rose garden with both climbing and bush roses. Mother took great pleasure in this. Another striking feature was a fine planting of azaleas that followed the driveway up the hill."

The Easter Sunday "Don't Quote Me" Column in the *Nashville Banner* included the following paragraph: "The Ridley Wills plan taking possession of their attractive place some bright day late in April. The Wills' place, you know, is the lovely new one on Curtis Wood Lane and those who have been through say it is perfect in every detail from the tiniest closet to the largest and most elaborate reception room. Jesse and Ellen Wills are going to be with them through the summer anyway, and have leased their apartment in Helena Court to Robert Lee Thomas and his bride, who was formerly Dot Ryan of Martin, Tennessee."

Naturally, lots of family members from Brownsville, Shelbyville, and Nashville came to see Far Hills. Included, of course, were Mann and Della. Upon seeing it, Mann, who had milk cows at home in Brownville, said, "Ridley, I wish I was your cow. It has the nicest house." The combination garage and barn was a lovely, brick building with a concrete floor.[51]

Although Jesse and Mamie Craig never lived at Far Hills, Mrs. Wills' sister, Miss Mamie Ely, did briefly. Between about 1927 and 1930, Mamie lived with Ridley and Jessie at their home on Louise Avenue. She moved there soon after her sister, Nell, died in 1927 because, at that point, Mr. Thompson broke up housekeeping and moved to the Polk Apartments on Seventh Avenue North. Mamie had lived with Nell and T. Leigh on State Street since 1922. After moving with Jessie and Ridley to Far Hills in 1930 and staying there for a short time, Mamie decided to move back to her hometown of Shelbyville, Tennessee. She did so and lived the rest of her life at the Dixie Hotel on the Shelbyville public square. Mr. Wills helped Mamie financially in accordance with the promise he made Jessie when they married in 1898. Ridley Wills II remembered seeing Miss Mamie and several elderly friends of hers when he was a child. His memory was of them having Sunday dinner at the Dixie Hotel, served by attentive African-American waiters.

Mamie Craig and Ted Clark were living at 220 Craighead Ave. when her parents moved to Far Hills. Wills, who bought the Craighead Avenue house for his daughter, still owned it at his death in 1949. The young couple had moved there in 1929. Shortly thereafter, the normally shy and unassertive Mamie Craig started the Little Garden Club. She and a circle of close friends, including Dot Tucker Coleman and Van Meter Blackie, would enjoy each other's company in the club for many years. In 1934, Ted left General Shoe and went back to running C.P. Clark Inc. at 2411 West End Avenue. There, Ted came up with the national advertising slogan "Four Roses and a Block of Ice" for Four Roses Kentucky Straight Bourbon Whiskey. In the decade following the repeal of prohibition in 1933, Four Roses became the most recognized name

---

51   "Dandy's Stories," Reminisces of Virginia Sturdivant Dodson.

Entrance Hall, Far Hills, 1936

Library, Far Hills, 1936

81

Court and Reflecting Pool, Far Hills, 1936

View of Far Hills residence, 1936

in the whiskey business. Ted's creativity helped make this possible.

The other half of Ridley Wills' game plan for his newfound wealth was more rational. It was to build and equip a hospital for his hometown of Brownsville, where his father had practiced medicine. Because of his own health problems, Wills was sensitive to the medical needs of the people there, both black and white, and knew how badly Haywood County needed a hospital. The lack of one forced people to go to Memphis or Jackson when hospitalization became a necessity. The new hospital, Ridley insisted, would not only be open to all the citizens of the county, but would have basement rooms for colored patients that were equal to those for whites. Although Wills assumed most, if not all, of the $100,000 cost of the 25-bed hospital, the gift was made in his name and that of his brother Mann. They would give the hospital in memory of their parents, Dr. and Mrs. William Thaddeus Wills.

The Wills brothers chose Estes Mann, a Memphis architect and cousin, as architect for the building. Mann presented plans for the 25-bed hospital in January 1930. The building was designed to supply medical, surgical and obstetrical services, along with lab and X-ray departments and quarters for student nurses who would be trained by the medical staff and, through affiliation with the Nashville General Hospital, would be able to take the state board examination to become registered nurses.[52]

Bids for construction of Haywood County Memorial Hospital were opened on May 2. Consolidated Contractors, of Memphis, was awarded the contract. The hospital would be built at 329 W. College St.

Construction of the Haywood County Memorial Hospital had progressed so well by October that Mrs. Dot Smallwood, a registered nurse and former superintendent of the Protestant Hospital in Nashville, was employed as the first superintendent and authorized to begin hiring key personnel for the new hospital. Ridley Wills knew her when he was a member of the Protestant Hospital board.

In December 1930, the medical staff for the Haywood County Memorial Hospital was organized in anticipation of the opening of the

---

52   The nurse training school closed in 1941. Brownsville-Haywood County Historical Society, *History of Haywood County*, 1989

hospital on January 6, 1931. The staff consisted of Dr. John Sevier, Dr. A. H. Sorrelle, Dr. Gill Mullherin, Dr. John Chambers, Dr. Glen Scott, Dr. W. D. Poston, Dr. W. R. Miller, Dr. D. I. Dupree, Dr. Fred Whitehurst, Dr. Leroy Gillespie, Dr. Guy Burton, Dr. G.W. Meux, Dr. John Munal, Dr. A.W. Livingston, Dr. Z. J. Scott, Dr. F. P. Hess, Dr. John Thornton Sr., Dr. T. C. Chapman, Dr. William Nash, Dr. L. W. Culbreath and Dr. R. T. Keeton. Sevier must have felt fulfilled, because he had, 15 years earlier, first pointed out to Ridley and Mann the desperate need for a hospital in Brownsville and solicited their interest in making that a reality. He was the Mann Wills' family physician for many years, and he looked after the medical needs of Mann and Della's daughters, Elizabeth and Harriette. In 1931, he removed the tonsils of Harriette's five-year-old son, Wills Oglesby, in the new Haywood County Memorial Hospital. Dr. Thornton, who was married to the former Mildred Taylor, was one of the county's most respected men. He would serve on the staff of the Haywood County Memorial Hospital from the time it opened until his death in 1971. Like most of his colleagues on the staff, he made house calls and delivered babies in the homes of many rural patients.

The first week in January, Ridley and Jesse drove to Brownsville for the dedication ceremony for the new Haywood County Hospital. *The Brownsville States-Graphic* of December 31, 1930, covered the event. "The present capacity of the hospital is 32 beds. This can be doubled if found necessary. The furnishings found throughout all the wards are of metal. On the main floor of the building are located the lobby, office, nurses and superintendent's quarters, doctors' consultation rooms, and sun parlor and rooms for patients. On each floor there are baths, running water, hot and cold, nurses' stations, sterilizers, public and hospital telephones. In the lobby, which is particularly attractive, there is a bronze tablet in which is inscribed the names of the donors and the subjects of the memorial. The offices and sun parlors are furnished with wicker and overstuffed leather chairs.

The nursery, operating rooms and a sun parlor are on the second floor. In the basement was a large kitchen, fully equipped with every sanitary and modern device, with no expense being spared here as well as in other departments of the modern structure. Another section of the basement will be devoted to the colored wards.

From the large underground basement where the heating and sterilizing equipment is furnished to the top of this imposing structure it has been constructed with but one thought, that of giving Haywood County one of the best institutions of its kind in towns this size anywhere in the United States,

Haywood County Memorial Hospital, 1930s

The city and county appropriated $10,000 annually for the hospital's operation. A board of trustees will have full control of the institution."

The dedication of the new Haywood County Memorial Hospital was at 10:30 a.m. in the auditorium of the Haywood County Courthouse. Every citizen of Haywood County was invited to attend. Many did, as well as dignitaries, friends and well-wishers from Nashville, Memphis and Jackson. The hospital, complete at a cost of more than $100,000, was given by Messrs. Mann Wills, of Brownville, and Ridley Wills, of Nashville, in memory of their parents, Dr. and Mrs. William Thaddeus Wills. Dr. Wills was described as having been a pioneer physician of Haywood County. During the ceremony, over which John T. Gray, Jr. presided, Mann Wills; Mrs. Dot Smallwood, hospital superintendent; Dr. J.H. Sevier; Judge John Rascoe Bond; and Dr. Rufus Fort spoke, and William Taylor Clarke, Mann's minister at the First Presbyterian Church, gave a prayer. Ridley Wills presented the hospital to the county while his niece, Miss Elizabeth Wills, then teaching English at Haywood County High School, accepted the hospital on behalf of the trustees while Dr. J. L. Edwards accepted on behalf of the physicians.

In his remarks, Ridley Wills insisted on Negroes being taken care of in the institution. "After all," he said, "They made it possible for us to build this hospital." Dr. Sevier interpreted this comment to mean, "Aunt Martha, with her prince consort, Uncle Alfred, was the real, if subconscious, cause for that provision." Martha and Alfred must have

The original board of trustees of Haywood County Memorial Hospital, 1932.
Left to Right: Willis B. Douglas, John D. Bomer, James Tipton, Elizabeth Wills,
Tom Mann, John T. Gray, Jr., and Nathan Tamm

been exceptional parents. Their son, a graduate of one of the best Negro schools in the state, went on to get degrees from the University of Pennsylvania and Chicago University, and to teach at Meharry Medical College.

The new fireproof structure was built on "the beautiful site of the old grammar school on West College Street that had burned." Following the dedication, the attendees toured the hospital where refreshments were served. The first patient to be admitted to Haywood County Memorial Hospital was Tom Halbrook who had surgery performed by Dr. Robert Mann, of Memphis, at no charge.[53]

During the hot summer of 1931, members of the Methodist and Presbyterian churches began to take box lunches of fried chicken and potato salad to the hospital after church on Sundays to eat in the lobby, the only room in town with air conditioning. This caused such a bottleneck that Smallwood had to request that the church members not come unless they had family members or friends hospitalized.

Each Christmas, beginning in 1931, Ridley would send Christmas checks to each member of the hospital staff. In the spring of 1934, the trustees of the hospital invited him to be the principal speaker at the third graduating exercise of the Haywood County Memorial Hospital nursing program, held Tuesday evening, June 5, 1934, at the First Presbyterian

---

53   Dr. Mann was a great uncle of Pat Mann, Jr.

Church. Wills accepted and drove down from Nashville on the 5th, where, after being introduced by his brother, he gave the address and presented diplomas to the four graduates of the nursing program. The insurance executive said, "The creation of this modern institution of mercy was the best investment I ever made, and the one that gave me more genuine satisfaction and pride than any other, and, if the time ever comes when it does not meet the needs of this community, I am ready to give the necessary financial aid to see that it does." Wills continued, saying that his only idea in giving this institution to his home county, whose people would always be dear to him, was to alleviate suffering and care for the unfortunate humanity. He paid high tribute to the ability and worth of the superintendent, Mrs. Dot Smallwood, the personnel of the institution, and the staff doctors who were giving full cooperation in its successful operation. The hospital, Wills said, had its inception some 15 years ago when he was invited to Brownsville by Dr. John Sevier to discuss the need of such an institution. The idea continued in his mind until it was possible for him to realize his ambition. He spoke in glowing terms of the worth of Sevier in his connection with the medical fraternity. After Wills' remarks, Dr. F.P. Hess delivered the address to the graduates. Smallwood concluded the ceremonies by presenting class pins to the four graduates.

The following November, Smallwood resigned as superintendent. Two weeks earlier, *The Brownsville States-Graphic* took notice of the changing of the guard. The article praised Smallwood with these words: "Her splendid executive ability and unselfish interest in her task has been largely responsible for the growth and development in usefulness of this agency of mercy which has served so well this community." The article also reported that the Board of Governors of the hospital had met and selected Mrs. Charlotte Lawson, of Nashville, as Smallwood's successor.

Chapter VIII

Marriage Bells and a New President, and Mann

When Mamie Craig delivered her first baby, Eleanor Clark, in March 1930, Papa Wills paid all of the medical bills, as he would for his grandchildren to come later. News of Eleanor's birth spread fast to Brownsville. On the 24th, Ridley's Aunt Eva Moore wrote him a letter of congratulations on his first grandchild. She enclosed "my note of $200 to you," and said she wanted to "pay you back or have my estate pay it." She also told Ridley that she owed Taylor Roofing Company on some roof work. This note was due, she wrote, on April 1, 1930. Moore, who took in boarders, also said, "We farmers have had a hard time last three or four years." She wrote that Mann had told her "not to sell any land yet." She spoke of her feelings for Ridley, saying, "You have been so sweet to me and I love you more than I can tell you. I thank God every day for your restoration of health," a reference to Ridley's periods of depression that had lasted, off and on from 1924 until 1929. Two days later, Ridley sent her $200 to cover the note due Taylor Roofing Company on April 1, 1930, and confirmed that she had agreed to repay the note to him on or before April 1, 1934. A few months later, Robert Sturdivant wrote Ridley about his Brownsville kinfolk. He spoke of Eva's habit of carrying a little snuff in her lower lip and, despite the hard times, the frequent invitations she extended to his family and others "to come git dinner with us," meaning her and her husband, William D. Moore, whom she affectionately called, "Mr. Mowe." At the time, Robert and Trousdale had four children – Robert Wills, born in 1914; Virginia, born in 1919; Trousdale, born in 1922; and Elizabeth "Bettie" Mann, born in 1925.

Meanwhile, Ridley and Jessie's son, Jesse, was in love with Ellen Buckner, an attractive and outgoing brunette, who was the youngest of three daughters of a respected and beloved Nashville physician, Dr. Matt Buckner, and his wife, Elizabeth Jackson Buckner. Jesse met Ellen, who was seven years his junior, at the railroad station in Knoxville in the fall of 1927. Ellen and her parents were spending the weekend there en route to New York, where they would embark on a tour around the world. Vanderbilt was playing the University of Tennessee that Saturday, and Ellen was among the VU supporters at the station to greet the arriving Vanderbilt players. She saw Jesse in the crowd and, having seen him in Nashville, spoke to him. When Ellen returned to Nashville in the summer of 1928, she asked Jesse if he would let a friend she had met on the trip use his membership to play golf at the Belle Meade County Club. Ellen had invited the young man to visit her in Nashville and didn't realize that Jesse would be jealous, but he was. That fall, Ellen recalled, "Jesse looked me up and we had our first date for the Harvest Ball."

Ellen was a member of the Girls' Cotillion Club and the Nashville Junior League. Jesse proposed to her in the spring of 1930 on the steps of her parents' new home in the Highlands of Belle Meade. Had Dr. and Mrs. Buckner known Ellen was planning to marry, they said they never would have moved from their smaller house on Terrace Place. Soon, Ellen and Jesse were nearly inundated with bridal parties. Among those who hosted pre-nuptial luncheons and dinners were Mr. and Mrs. Runcie Clements, who gave a luncheon for them at the Belle Meade Country Club, and Mamie Craig Clark who gave a bridge luncheon for Ellen at her home on Craighead. Mr. and Mrs. Wills gave the rehearsal dinner at the Centennial Club, where Mrs. Wills was a member and, in 1937, a director.

Dr. James I. Vance married Jesse and Ellen at the First Presbyterian Church on June 17, 1930. This happened only a few weeks before Jesse's parents moved from Louise Avenue to Far Hills. Ellen's sisters, Elizabeth Maddin and Mary Harding Ragland, and her future sister-in-law, Mamie

Ellen McClung Buckner in her wedding dress, June 1930.

Craig, served as her matrons of honor. The maid of honor was Miss Elizabeth Bryan of Nashville. Ellen's other bridesmaids were Gertrude Lewis, Ann Leslie Nichol, Laura McAlister, Frances Duke, Rachel Buntin and Frances Gerhardt of Murfreesboro. At the last minute, Rachel dropped out – supposedly because of her grandmother's death. Ellen later heard that Rachel did so because she had a golf game that seemed more important than the wedding. Eleanor Alsup, a distant cousin from Washington, stepped in as a substitute bridesmaid. Bob Worke Jr. was Jesse's' best man, while Ted Clark, Stuart Ragland, John Maddin, Vernon Sharp Jr., Laird Smith, Jimmy Waller, George Henry Tyne, Miller Manier and Robert Orr III served as groomsmen.

Because the Buckner's home at 1111 Belle Meade Blvd. was not as large as "Journey's End," the Ellendale Avenue home of Ellen's sister and brother-in-law, Elizabeth and John Maddin, her wedding reception was held there. Following it, someone drove Jesse and Ellen to Union Station – followed by the entire wedding party who saw them off on the night train for New York. There they boarded the *S. S. Transylvania* for a six-week honeymoon in Europe. After landing in Glasgow, they motored down through the English Lake District. They then visited, London, Paris and Lake Como and witnessed the Passion play in the Bavarian village of Oberammergau before returning home. Upon their return, they set up housekeeping in the Helena Court, built in 1930, on Belle Meade Boulevard.

Despite the Great Depression, Ridley and National Life were doing amazingly well. In January 1931, Ridley's friends in Brownsville read in the *States-Graphic* that he had succeeded Mr. Craig as president of the National Life and Accident Insurance Company. They rejoiced over their native son's achievement and thought Ridley Wills must be one of the richest men in America. Because Craig was not ready to retire, the National Life Board created a new position of chairman of the board and elected him to that post. Part of Ridley's routine every workday morning, as president, was to walk through the home office and speak to every employee.

To close out a difficult year with a positive finish, the three principal officers of National Life – Mr. Craig, Mr. Wills and Mr. Clements – divided the company's three territories among themselves. Ridley drew the Southern Territory with 36 district offices in Alabama, Georgia and Tennessee. Every week, he scrutinized reports showing the increase of each district's debit, the percentage of collections and the amount of Ordinary insurance sold. He called each manager weekly to challenge, encourage or admonish him and also wrote letters to each district manager. The campaign and personal attention from top management worked. National Life closed 1931 with the largest amount of assets in its history. Assets grew from $29.5 million in 1930 to more than $32 million in 1931, while insurance in force increased from $315 million in 1930 to more than $321 million in 1931.

In May 1931, Ridley's son, Jesse, and his wife, Ellen, had a baby named Jesse Ely Wills Jr. It was clear from the time of his birth that he would not survive. Baby Jesse died the next day. Because Mrs. Wills was naturally upset, Ridley thought it would do her some good if she took her only grandchild, Eleanor Clark, to Atlantic City that summer. Mrs. Wills did so, taking along a maid to look after the baby. They stayed at the exclusive Haddon Hall Hotel on the boardwalk.

On August 1, 1931, Ridley Wills wrote Mrs. W. S. Smartt, agent for the Woman's Club of Nashville, outlining his proposal to sell his house at 217 Louise Ave. to the Woman's Club of Nashville. He wrote he would do so for a price of $16,000 with $3,000 payable in cash, and $500 payable on the first days of June 1933, 1934, 1935 and 1936; $1,000 on the first days of June 1937 through 1946; and $1,000 on June 1, 1947. The sale would include stoves, radiator coverings, awnings, light fixtures and all other fixtures installed in the house. Finally, he asked for a response by noon on August 4, 1931. Mrs. J.B. Henderson, president, accepted the proposition.

During the Depression, the club had a hard time making the payments. As was so characteristic of him, Wills agreed to reduce the indebtedness by nearly 50 percent. Even this was not sufficient help, as when Ridley died in 1949, the Women's Club still owed him $7,381. In 2008, the house was widely known as the home of Jimmy Kelly's Restaurant.

Highlights of 1932 were National Life's Pearl Jubilee, held in May, to celebrate the company's 30th anniversary; the October 5 completion of WSM's new radio tower on Concord Road south of Brentwood; and

National Life's Pearl Jubilee Celebration, May 1932.
The company founders and their wives pictured left to right: C.R. Clements, Mrs. Clements,
Mrs. C. A. Craig, C. A. Craig, Ridley Wills, Mrs. Thomas Tyne, Mrs. Ridley Wills,
Thomas Tyne, Dr. Rufus E. Fort, and Mrs. Fort.

the October 22 birth of a healthy grandson, Matthew Buckner Wills.

At the Pearl Jubilee, the company's five founders and their wives posed for a photograph behind a huge floral design in the shape of a heart or shield with five ribbons radiating out from a bow in the center. On each ribbon was the name of one of the founders,

At the Pearl Jubilee, President Wills spoke on the company's history and lauded the contributions of Mr. Clements, Mr. E.B. Craig, Mr. Tyne, and Dr. Fort. As for the originator of the idea to purchase the company, C.A. Craig, Wills called him "the finest president any insurance company ever had for nearly 30 years, and the finest Chairman of the Board any insurance company has ever had for a little more than a year." Wills said he wished he could live those 30 years over again, from their start in 1902 with $33,000 in assets to 1932 when "we now have more than $33 million of assets." That evening, 15 men received 30-year pins. Despite working closely with each other for 30 years, and their being warm, personal friends, Wills invariably greeted Craig as "Mr. Craig" rather than as "Neely" on formal occasions, such as the Pearl Jubilee. Craig, in turn, frequently used the formal "Mr. Wills," rather than "Ridley

The new WSM tower stood 878 feet high and was heralded as America's tallest radio tower. Indeed, it stood 323 feet higher than the Washington Monument. In the decades to come, aspiring country musicians headed for Nashville and, hopefully, stardom, on U.S. 31A, would get chills as they gazed at the tower that symbolized the strength of WSM-The Air Castle of the South.

While brother Ridley was going strong at National Life, Mann and Della Wills still lived modestly at 506 Park Ave. in Brownsville's 4th Ward. Their home was a one-story frame house with a front and side porch, dining room, parlor, library, kitchen with breakfast area, three bedrooms, bath, pantry, and small back porch. Mann was still practicing law at his office on the public square, walking to work five and sometimes six days a week. Unfortunately, his law practice was anything but lucrative during the Depression. To supplement his income, Mann had been, for some time, making loans on homes and farms all over West Tennessee, advertising low rates and quick service. Unfortunately, in the early '30s, many of his clients missed payments on their loans and lost their land and homes through foreclosure. Despite the fact that Mann had little money, he always was helping those less fortunate than he. This included giving away some of his cows to Brownsville's needy.

Mann's greatest satisfaction came from the Sunday School class he had taught at First Presbyterian Church since 1906. In 1935, a reporter for the *Jackson Sun* met Mann, whom he knew, in downtown Jackson. He asked about the news in Brownsville and Haywood County. Mann replied, "Well the biggest news in Haywood County is that I had 150 people in my Sunday School class last Sunday." The reporter listened to what Wills had to say and then tried to turn the discussion toward the general improvements in the county, including the public schools. He failed. Wills expanded further on his class, saying, "It embraces all creeds and those of no creed and is the biggest thing in Haywood County." In the summers, Mann let his grandsons attend the Sunday School class. Herbert and Wills Oglesby had the honor of holding their grandfather's pocket watch during the class and telling him when it was time to stop. Wills did not always heed their warning.

Mann Wills' Sunday School class at First Presbyterian Church, Brownsville, TN, 1929. Ridley Wills II is seated holding his daughter, Tookie, on the first step. To Ridley's right is his mother, Della Womack Wills, wearing a light-colored blouse. Her daughter, Elizabeth Wills, is the other lady seated on the second step. Elizabeth's father, Mann Wills, is seated, with hat in his lap, on the third step between Elizabeth and Della.

Mann also loved fishing and, annually took his class on fishing trips to his camp on the Hatchie River, to the Boy Scout Camp at Sunkist Beach adjacent to Reelfoot Lake, or to Open Lake in Lauderdale County. On the weekend of June 21–23, 1933, Mann hosted a fish fry for his class on Reelfoot Lake. He invited Ridley, and planned for him to be quartered with Della and Elizabeth Wills at Will Frierson's furnished cottage. Mann told Ridley that it had "comfortable beds, good water, electric lights and a toilet." In June 1935, 35 members of Wills' class, including Dee Evans, an expert fisherman, camped with him at Sunkist Beach. The cost was $2 per person. Mann brought a ham and 20 chickens to feed the crowd. Some years, Mann, who was a Ruling Elder and had been chairman of the Board of Deacons for two decades at First Presbyterian, would host a banquet for his Sunday School class.

Mann hosted other fishing trips for his friends. In May 1933, he and four others went out on Reelfoot and caught more than 100 fish. A Democrat, Mann also was a prohibitionist. On May 29, 1933, he spoke to 500 people at Harmony on the issue. He told his audience that he was "in the dry campaign up to my neck" and that "I am drinking prune juice." A few weeks later, Ridley wrote Mann, advising him "to vote as you think you should and not worry about the result." Ridley said he felt certain "Tennessee will vote strongly for repeal." On July 7, 1933, the 21st Amendment, which provided for the repeal of prohibition, was ratified.

Mann Wills spoke at the Brownsville Rotary Club twice in 1934. An interesting and entertaining speaker, Mann was so well received the first time that the club asked him to come back on April 29 and talk about some of the prominent early settlers in Haywood County. Mann did so with wit and humor. When Gov. Hill McAlister came to town in July to kick off his reelection campaign in West Tennessee, he and his wife were guests of Mann and Della for lunch. On November 3, during the general election, Mann spoke on the courthouse steps on behalf of all the Democratic party nominees. On Friday, the *States-Graphic* publicized the event, saying, "Mr. Wills is a forceful speaker with a genuine interest in the success of the Democratic party in the election next Tuesday. He has many friends throughout the county who will be delighted to hear him."

Although Mann didn't talk about it much, he was constantly worried about his brilliant but unreliable son, Ridley II, who, failing to get the position as state librarian, had not found himself. Ridley, his wife, the former Luella Whitehead Wilson, of Jackson, Tennessee, whom he married in 1923, and their five children, Luella "Tookie" Wills, William Ridley "Bill" Wills III, Andrew Mann "Andy" Wills, David Womack Wills and John Thomas Thaddeus Wills lived at various times, in Brownsville, Memphis, Nashville and Jackson, Tennessee, where Ridley got a job with Western Auto selling bicycles. When they lived in Brownsville, Ridley had no job and lived in "a little bitty house" that Mann rented for him. To get nourishing meals, the children would walk to their grandparents' house, as Luella didn't like to cook. When he was a reporter for the *Memphis Commercial Appeal*, Ridley was paid $75 per week and wrote a popular column titled "Rambling with Ridley" that often dealt with hunting and fishing. That job ended when Ridley decided that Boss Crump ought to leave Memphis and that he would help run him out of town. Instead, Ridley got run out of Memphis.

While he was with the *Nashville Banner* from 1935 to 1936, Ridley often had lead articles. He, Luella and their children lived most of that time in a nice two-story house at 1137 Howard Ave. in Inglewood. One day, when Ridley was in a good mood, he told his family about a joke he and some friends in the legislature played on the lieutenant governor earlier that day. A state senator wired the lieutenant governor's chair for electricity so they could shock him by turning on the power. The joksters then paid a small, ragged girl to come in the Senate Chamber crying for her father. According to Ridley's son, David, the presiding officer in the Senate called for silence and asked that, if the little girl's father was present, would he please stand up. They then turned the power on to the lieutenant governor's seat and he, of course, jumped up. Everybody but the lieutenant governor seemed to enjoy the joke.[54]

Later, the Wills moved to a small apartment at 1910A Broadway in Nashville before moving back to Brownsville.

By 1933, Ridley was an alcoholic. The disease gradually gained control of his life, causing him to lose his newspaper jobs and his car, embarrassing and alienating most of his relatives, taking an enormous toll on his children and wrecking his marriage.[55] In August 1937, a year after Mann's death, Ridley and Luella moved to Cincinnati, where he was promised a job as assistant editor of a newspaper. The children's grandmother, Della Wills, broke the news to her grandchildren that they would not be accompanying their parents to Ohio. Instead, she said that she had found a very nice place for Bill, Andy, David and John to board. This turned out to be a foster home in Smyrna, Tennessee, run by Mr. and Mrs. Lee. The boys would become wards of the State of Tennessee, whose Welfare Department would pay the Lees for their room and board. The family decided that Tookie would stay with her Aunt Bee (Elizabeth Wills).

Trousdale's husband, Bob Sturdivant, drove the boys to Smyrna on August 15, 1937. The boys remained there for six seven months when their mother and sister arrived to take them to a new life in Jacksonville, Florida. There, they saw their father briefly. One Monday, after supper,

---

54   David Womack Wills, *Depression Daze*, privately published, 2001, p. 10.

55   Luella divorced Ridley twice but both times remarried him.

Luella got her children together and told them that their father would not be coming back for a while. She said he had entered a Veterans Hospital in St. Petersburg called Bay Pines to check on a burn he got in his throat during World War I. Doctors at Bay Pines diagnosed his problem as post-traumatic stress syndrome, related to his battle experiences in the war. Ridley's children would not see their father again for four years. Despite their difficult childhoods and a lack of financial support, all the Wills children managed to attend college.[56] Their father, Ridley, died at Bay Pines June 25, 1957.

---

56   Luella "Tookie" Wills Willard graduated from Stetson College with a B.A. degree and later worked with the National Security Agency. Before her death in 1998, she lived for many years in western North Carolina. Bill received an architectural degree from Georgia Tech in 1949. He later did graduate work at La Sorbonne and worked as an architect in London and Paris where he mysteriously disappeared in 1967. Andy went in the U.S. Navy during World War II and was adrift in the ocean for two days after his ship was sunk. After the war, he went to Stetson for three years and spent his career as an explosives engineer for the military. David Womack held a bachelor's degree and two master's degrees. After retiring from the Air Force, he taught in high school and at a local community college in Lake Mary, Fla. Thad attended Stetson for one year, the University of Georgia for two years, and spent two years studying at a division of the College of William and Mary. Early in his business career, he worked with the Social Security Administration in Baltimore, where he met his wife, Virginia Cheney. They lived for many years in Versailles, Kentucky, where he died in 2008.

CHAPTER IX

HELPING WHERE HE COULD

Jessie and Ridley Wills were so happy for Jesse and Ellen when she delivered a healthy baby boy in October 1932, only 17 months after they lost their first son, Jesse Ely Wills, Jr. They named the little boy Matthew Buckner Wills for his maternal grandfather, Dr. Matthew Gardner Buckner.

After New Year 1933, Mr. and Mrs. Wills, their daughter, Mamie Craig, her two-year-old granddaughter, Eleanor, and a maid, went by train to Miami Beach to escape the worst of the winter in Nashville. Ridley stayed only for the weekend before returning to work on Sunday the 8th. Everyone else stayed at the Lincoln Hotel until January 24. Mr. Wills found the trip home "long and tiresome," and said he didn't see anybody he knew until the train reached Chattanooga. On reaching home Monday morning, Ridley found everything in fine shape with all the servants there. He wrote Jessie on Tuesday to assure her he was fine and was "being a good boy." "This afternoon," Ridley told Jessie he was going to see Jesse and his baby son, Matt Buckner Wills, then 3 months old. He also was anxious to see Jesse and Ellen's new house, Meade Haven, two houses beyond Dr. and Mrs. Buckner's home on Belle Meade Boulevard. Ridley also told Jessie that he had talked to Ted Clark, who said he talked to Mamie Craig "the same day I left." Ridley expressed the hope that Mamie Craig, who was two months pregnant, "continues to improve."

Ridley was well taken care of while Jessie was in Miami Beach, Sometimes he would have dinner with Jesse and Ellen, and, at least on one occasion, with Dr. and Mrs. Fort at their palatial home, Fortland, on Riverside Memorial Drive in East Nashville. One night, Leigh Thompson spent the night with Ridley at Far Hills. He took a weekend trip to Brownsville, and upon returning he wrote Jessie, "Everybody in Brownsville is well though much afflicted with poverty."

At a Monroe Harding Children's Home board meeting on January 19, Ridley spoke to Governor McAlister about his nephew Ridley's chances at getting the state librarian position. When the governor said

Meade Haven, Belle Meade Boulevard, 1934

he had strong competition from Mrs. John Trotwood Moore and Mrs. Benton McMillan, the widow of the late governor, Ridley asked Hill to secure Ridley a place "that has to do with keeping the state archives." While his wife was in Florida, Ridley kept busy as ever. In addition to long days at National Life, he traded correspondence with the recorder for the town of Whiteville, Tennessee, regarding City of Whiteville bonds he held and on which the city was delinquent in paying interest. In February, he declined Chancellor Kirkland's request that he serve on the Vanderbilt Hospital board, calling the chancellor's attention to the fact that "Mr. C R. Clements of our organization is a member of this board." Mann Wills' sister-in-law, Hattie Thornton, wrote Ridley in early February, asking him "if you could find something in your big business world for my young son, Joe, who graduates from high school the first of June 1933. Ridley responded quickly, saying, "I will bear Joe in mind for work at National Life but the hiring situation is not in the least encouraging."[57] On February 10, Ridley asked George Morris, the secretary of Governor McAlister, to put in a good word for his nephew, Ridley Wills, who desperately wanted the job of state librarian. On

---

57   Mr. Wills could not find a job for Joseph Richard Thornton, Jr. at National Life. After attending the University of Tennessee, Joe became the first in his generation to leave the farm for a job in town. He married, served in World War II, became a Shriner, a businessman and an active member of the First United Methodist Church in Covington, Tennessee.

February 11, Ridley wrote the Honorable Joseph W. Byrns, congressman from Tennessee, asking him to appoint Mrs. Jennie Patton Fort, wife of Charles Fort, of Adams, Tennessee, postmistress at Adams. Charles was kin to Dr. Rufus Fort. Four days later, Ridley wrote Macon Thornton to say that he had arranged, through Cecil Sims, a Nashville attorney, for Mann Wills to be appointed attorney in connection with the failure of the Stanton, Tennessee, bank. Mann wrote Ridley on February 22 to thank him for his help in getting him appointed to file a bill to formally declare the Stanton Bank bankrupt. Mann said he expected to be paid $1,000 for the work he did for the Stanton Bank and $2,000 for legal work he did for the First State Bank in Brownsville, which also failed. He asked Ridley for a $200 loan to tide him over until he received those checks. Ridley responded in two days, enclosing a National Life check for $500 made out to Mann Wills for work he had done on some suits in Chancery Court. Ridley said he knew about the First State Bank failing and expressed the hope that something could be worked out with the depositors. He added, "I realize the $2,000 in stock that I own is worthless." The day before, Ridley turned down a request from a former National Life employee in Louisville for a $25 loan, saying, "I am so much crowded along this line at this time that it is impossible for me to accommodate you in this matter." He received a thank-you letter the same day from an old friend to whom he had lent or given $200. A few days later, Mann wrote Ridley thanking him for the $500. Mann said, "The money and future fees will enable me, Della and our son Ridley and his family to get along economically." For the next several months, Ridley continued trying to get his nephew the state librarian job. He was unsuccessful. Mrs. John Trotwood Moore, who had much more experience than Ridley, got the position.

Some weeks later, on March 17, 1933, Jessie was admitted as a member of the North Carolina Society of the Colonial Dames of America. In applying for membership, she had proved her lineal descent from Eley Eley, Lieutenant of Hartford County, North Carolina, in 1772, who died in Logan County, Kentucky, in 1813.[58]

March 1933 also saw National Life hire a 25-year-old advertising

---

58   Alternative spellings of his name were Eli and Ely.

man named Ed Kirby. "Less than a month into Kirby's tenure, *Our Shield* began to preview new WSM shows he was developing "to help 2,500 Shield men." The first was called the National Life Variety Show. President Wills wrote in an open letter to the sales force: "I am being made happier than in a long time by the fine way in which our radio station WSM is being tied in with the work of the Shield Man…It appears to me that Mr. Kirby, under the direction of Mr. E.W. Craig mainly, has begun a fine work." He, Mr. Craig and Mr. Clements praised Kirby's resourcefulness in making the Shield name more relevant and in promoting National Life business.

One of the families in Brownsville that was kind to Ridley's mother after Dr. Wills died was the parents or grandparents of Miss Edith Myers. This young woman had been confined to Watauga Sanitarium at Ridgetop, Tennessee, since the summer of 1930. Mr. Wills paid her bills, $10 a week, for several years, either as a loan or a gift, and occasionally visited her.

The requests for help that crossed Ridley Wills' desk at National Life never seemed to abate. In March, he received a letter from his beloved pastor, James I. Vance, asking his help in "finding a place for Weldon Phillips at National Life. On March 24, he wrote Congressman Joe Byrns, recommending Green Benton for a government job. Byrns replied that he was a close friend of Benton's but could not help him as Benton was too old to take the Civil Service examination. On March 28, Ridley wrote Cordell Hull recommending Allen V. McDonald, of Waco, Texas, for the position of minister of the Irish Free State. McDonald was a friend of Mrs. Bert Moore Scales, who grew up in Brownsville, Tennessee.

In early April, Nashvillian Willard Tirrill, chairman of the Finance Committee Central Unemployment Relief Committee, asked Ridley for $400 to give part-time work to 400 unemployed men at a truck garden adjacent to the Confederate Soldiers Home at The Hermitage. Ridley sent him a check for $50. In a thank you letter, Tirrill said, "We only wish there were a lot more like Mr. W.R. Wills, for we know he is one whose heart is always ready to respond." Ridley was on the budget committee for First Presbyterian Church that submitted, on April 10, a proposed budget of $22,588. This included a salary of $6,000 for Vance and one of $3,000 for his associate pastor, Dr. Thomas Barr.

By 1933, President Roosevelt's New Deal was in full swing. In a letter to Ridley, dated April 17, Mann Wills said, "Mr. Roosevelt has pulled the wagon out of the mud, but where in hell it will go, I don't know as I am old fashioned enough not to believe in the government getting in all kinds of business. I look for the government to put up hot dog stands in a few years." Two months later, Roosevelt's Industrial Recovery Act (NIRA) became law. It authorized the president to regulate business in the interest of promoting fair competition, supporting prices and competition, creating jobs for the unemployed and stimulating the U.S. economy to recover from the Depression. Although the NIRA was not strongly supported by leading American businessmen, National Life's Executive Committee adopted a resolution in July supporting it, In his "Thursday letter" to the field force, Mr. Wills announced the decision, writing "In signing this, we mean just what the NIRA agreement said, and intend to live up to it's provisions 100 percent just as we intend, when we execute a policy contract, to carry out its provisions 100 percent."

Three years later, Ridley elaborated on his political views in a letter to the editor of a Nashville newspaper. He wrote, "While I do not agree with many of the things apparently sponsored by the Democratic Administration, I do approve of some of their enterprises, such as the Banking Act, the Securities Registration, and some other minor matters. I heartily disapprove of the AAA, the Wagner Labor Disputes Bill, the Guffey Act, and other similar statutes. I believe that the proper course is for Democrats to stay in the party and work toward eliminating those who are now pointing toward socialism."

Three months later, Robert L. Garner, a senior officer at Guaranty Trust in New York City, responded to a letter Ridley wrote him. Garner said that, although he was a Democrat, "there is no Democrat running for president this year." He then said: "It is hard for me to see how a man in the insurance business, founded on the protection of property rights, dependent on thrift and fair return on capital, makes a virtue of improvidence, could support a continuous policy of operating in the red. Perfectly honestly, do you like or trust the New Deal?" Ridley responded: "I am perfectly honest in saying to you that, on the whole, I like and trust the New Deal, not meaning to have you understand that a great part of what they have done really meets with my approval. The whole picture as it presents itself to me causes a definite conviction that it is best for America that Roosevelt be reelected."

In the 1936 general election, Roosevelt would defeat Kansas Governor Alf Landon, winning 60.8 percent of the vote and carrying every state except Maine and Vermont.

Despite the flood of requests Ridley received for financial help, the Depression did not hammer Nashville as hard as it did more industrialized Southern cities or small towns such as Brownsville. Nevertheless, the city did suffer enormously, with black areas particularly hard hit. In 1933, Fisk University trustees faced the real possibility that the school might not survive. Unless they balanced the school's budget that year, they stood to lose a foundation grant of $100,000. Despite having cut their budget by 20 percent, achieving a balanced budget seemed impossible in August. Fortunately, two community leaders, Jeff Gray Jr., a Nashville businessman, and Ridley Wills, president of National Life, agreed to co-chair a $37,500 campaign to benefit Fisk University and the Southern YMCA College, a Nashville institution, led by the progressive reformer Willis D. Weatherford. The five-day drive in late September, if successful, would net $25,000 for Fisk and $12,500 for the YMCA Graduate School, which was also running a budget deficit. Gray and Wills worked with many others, including the aged Negro leader, J.C. Napier, who headed the Negro Section of the drive for Fisk.[59] Realizing that he needed to set an example by making a lead gift, Ridley Wills wrote a check for $1,000, designating $333.33 to the YMCA Graduate School and $666.66 to the Fisk campaign. He got another $500 from one of his associates at National Life.

On October 1, *The Nashville Tennessean* announced that the drive was $12,000 short. Wills said, "We are going ahead until all the money is raised." Fisk President Thomas E. Jones was just as insistent. He was emphatic, saying: "We are going to get this money. Nashville has too much at stake in this campaign not to be able to announce to the great foundations that she is not unmindful of the many millions that have been invested here and the millions more that some Southern city is

---

59   *The Nashville Tennessean*, September 24, 1933.

going to receive for educational purposes."

One person who followed the campaign with great interest was John Knox, a young cousin of Wills. Knox, who was minister of the chapel on the Fisk campus, wrote "Cousin Ridley," on September 27, to tell him "how much I appreciate what you are doing this week for our institution." Knox said that, ever since moving to Nashville, he had wanted to know Ridley better but had not followed up because he knew how controversial it was for a white minister to live with his family on a black campus ministering to black students, and he didn't want to embarrass him.

Knox continued, "My cousins, except for the immediate family, have generally rather deeply deplored my being here. In the case of Lois, my wife, not even her immediate family can be excepted." He said only his great aunt Eva Moore in Brownville gave him "a friendly word." He said, "To find you showing in such a conspicuous and convincing way your faith in what we are about is naturally a source of peculiar happiness to me." Knox said he wanted Ridley to meet his wife and baby and would be honored if Ridley could find the time to stop by his house, but, if that were inconvenient, he would be honored to bring his wife and baby for a short visit in Ridley's office.

Fisk did not close, and President Jones was grateful to Gray, Wills and their campaign team. In a 1936 Christmas letter to Wills, Jones reflected, "As I look back over 1936, one of the bright spots was your friendship." He said that on the occasional times when he saw Ridley: "I never failed to find [in Ridley] a spirit of genuine good will and cordiality. We do not forget the service you rendered Fisk three years ago when a great deal depended on our maintaining our program and staying out of debt. I wish that you could visit Fisk more often, for the ideals which you seem to hold are those upon which Fisk University was founded and through which it has and must continue to serve the nation." He wished Mr. Wills a very Merry Christmas and a Happy New Year.

The previous fall, O.B. Taylor, a Knoxville physician and surgeon, wrote Wills to thank him for a generous gift of $50 that National Life gave to a Negro Hospital in Knoxville. Taylor said that in making the request of National Life, he was not unmindful "of your liberal past history in dealing with members of our racial group." He then said that he personally knew of no insurance company operating in Knoxville that he could recommend with more genuine sincerity than National Life and Accident. Taylor knew Mr. Andrews, National Life's representative in Knoxville and found him to be very able. He said the news of National Life's gift "shall spread city-wide here."

At the end of June 1933, Jessie and Ridley traveled by train to Lynchburg, Virginia, to attend the wedding of Dr. Fort's son, Rufus E. Fort Jr., and Agnes Stokes, of Lynchburg. Ridley had intended to go on to Trevalin, Virginia, where the Wills once lived, but did not do so because it was farther than he anticipated. Once home, Jessie checked on her pregnant daughter, Mamie Craig, who was expecting anytime. Her daughter, Phoebe Clark, was born July 14. at St. Thomas Hospital, delivered by Dr. R.O. Tucker.

Early in August, Ridley and several friends, probably including Neely Craig, drove to Open Lake, arriving by supper on Wednesday, August 9. His Aunt Eva hoped he would stop in Brownsville either on the way down or on the way back Sunday. Of course, Mann expressed interested in Ridley's new grandbaby. Ridley said, "Phoebe is very fine but she will have a hard time coming up to the first one (Eleanor)." With Ridley and Mann on the fishing outing were an equal number of men from Brownsville and Nashville. Everything went smoothly until Ridley fell and broke his arm. He and Mann drove to Haywood County Memorial Hospital to have his arm set. There, Dr. John Munal set Ridley's arm and put it in a splint. The hospital did not want to charge Wills, who after all was their patron saint, but he insisted on mailing them a check for $50 once he got home. On Monday morning, at the office, Ridley asked Dr. Fort to examine his arm. Fort did so and said no further action was necessary in that his arm should heal itself and he could take the splint off after three weeks. Mann, concerned about his brother, sent both Ridley and Neely Craig watermelons, and thanked Ridley for making the outing possible.

Ridley's arm caused him little pain and he healed in time to take Jessie, their granddaughter, Eleanor, and a colored nurse by train to Atlantic City on August 6. A week earlier, Wills had written the manager of the Haddon Hall Hotel asking that he reserve the same connecting rooms they had two years earlier. Ridley and Jessie would stay in the larger room that had two single beds, a circulating fan, a radio and a bath, while the nurse and three-and-a-half-year-old Eleanor would sleep in the adjoining room that had a single bed and a child's bed. That room also had a circulating fan and bath. With the Wills on the trip were Mr. and Mrs. Tom Tyne. Part of the two weeks the Wills were at Atlantic City, Wills and Tyne attended an insurance meeting.

When Ridley returned to his office on the twenty-first, he found the usual pile of letters. One was from Robert "Spud" Weaver, a good friend of Jesse's at Vanderbilt and in the Phi Delta Theta Fraternity. Wills had given Weaver a job as an agent in Memphis, not far from Weaver's home in Tupelo. Spud had read about Wills' accident in the *Commercial Appeal* and was writing to express concern over that and to thank Wills for "your many kindnesses to me and mine."[60]

After retiring from National Life, T. Leigh Thompson, whose deceased first wife, Nellie, was Jessie's beloved sister, married Mrs. Dee Waller Turrentine. Mr. and Mrs. Thompson lived at his beloved Wild Rose Farm in Marshall County during the spring, summer and fall and went to their winter home in St. Petersburg during the winter. Ridley thought Leigh's marriage was fine. Jessie thought he should not have remarried and severed all social relationships with him. Disregarding this, Jesse, who still loved Uncle T. Leigh, would later dedicate a poem to him. The poem, published in *Early and Late,* has the title, "Salute to T. L. T. 1862–1954."

Tragedy struck Nashville, and Ridley personally, on September 17, 1933, when 61-year-old Nashville hardware distribution president Sheffield Clark was murdered in a New Orleans hotel while on a business trip there. Until his death, Sheffield and his wife, Idella, lived at 2208 Patterson St., three houses down from where Ridley and Jessie lived from 1906 until 1913. The Clarks were fellow members of First Presbyterian Church. Frustrated, as were all of Sheffield's friends, by his murder, Ridley wrote New Orleans Attorney General Bernard Cooke, who would prosecute the suspected murderer, to say "that the people of Nashville are deeply interested in this case" because of the respect they

---

60   When Robert "Spud" Weaver died, Jesse Wills wrote a poem about his college friend entitled *On Hearing of the Death of a Friend.* The poem is in *Conversation Piece and Other Poems,* published in 1965.

had for Clark. Wills added, "I have never known a finer husband, father, or neighbor than he was."[61]

On October 10, Mr. and Mrs. Wills and Mr. and Mrs. Stevenson were in Chicago for a meeting of National Life field people. While the men were in a meeting, Mrs. Wills cut her forehead when the Yellow Cab in which she was riding had a wreck. She was taken to the American Hospital where X-rays were taken and she was given stitches to close the wound. Before they returned to Nashville on October 15, Mr. Wills retained Chicago attorney William Wentzel to represent him. On October 20, he wrote Wentzel to say that there had been no complications from the injury and that, apparently, Mrs. Wills would have only a slight scar. He instructed his attorney to "be entirely reasonable with the Yellow Cab Company" and that he simply wanted to be reimbursed for the expenses she incurred. The case was settled in January for $225.

Soon after the Wills got home, Mr. E.F. Arrowsmith, manager of one of the Chicago district offices, wrote Wills to speak about "the world of good your meeting here did for my men." He also said that lots of National Life policyholders in Chicago could not pick up WSM and wondered if they could exchange programs with a Chicago station.

In October, Mann invited C.A. Craig to a fishing trip in West Tennessee. Craig declined because he was under the care of a physician at the time. Mann responded by saying, "I am extending the invitation at your pleasure and, when you come, I will show you how a poor boy can entertain a man he really likes." Changing subjects, Mann said, "Things are picking up here and you will see the results in the remittances." Mann was referring to his collecting interest on mortgage loans National Life had in West Tennessee.

Vanderbilt played Tennessee in Knoxville that fall, and Ridley and Jessie were there with friends. They spent Friday and Saturday nights at A.J. Huff's Mountain View Hotel in Gatlinburg. While they enjoyed the fall colors, the game was a disappointment as Beattie Feathers stormed to three touchdowns leading Tennessee to a 33-6 victory. It was the worst defeat by Tennessee since the series started in 1892. On Saturday

---

61   Twenty-six-year-old Louis K. Neu, of Savannah, Georgia, confessed to the crime. He later pled innocent by way of insanity. *The Nashville Tennessean*, September 21, 1933.

Mr. and Mrs. Ridley Wills with family members in their Dudley Stadium box at the Vanderbilt-Chattanooga football game, September 27, 1930. Mamie Craig (Mrs. C. P.) Clark is in the front row, third from the left. To her right are Ellen Buckner and Jesse Ely Wills. In the second row of the box, Jessie Ely Wills is the third person from the left. To her right is Ridley Wills.

morning, Wills met with the field force at the Knoxville office. Before leaving for Knoxville, Ridley paid the night watchman at Far Hills $17.50 for work done in October. On returning to the office on Monday, Ridley got a bill from Mrs. C.A. Breast, wife of the owner of the Dixie Hotel in Shelbyville, for dining room expenses for Jessie's sister, Mamie and four of her friends. True to the word he gave Jessie when they became engaged 35 years earlier, Ridley paid the bill.

Ridley had been a member of the Belle Meade Country Club for many years, but he did not play golf or tennis. He and Jessie ate dinner there on occasion, usually on Saturday night. In December 1933 his dues were $12.08. Ridley's cousin, Sarah Shaw of Brownsville, wrote him in December 1933 after Macon Thornton, acting as an agent for National Life, told her that the insurance company would not rent her what was known as the Shaw Place for another year. Wills spoke to someone in the Mortgage Loan Department before writing her that his policy was not to interfere with that department's decisions on renting company property.

In 1933, Ridley and Jessie gave $7,676.66 to charities. Their five largest gifts were $2,750 to the Community Chest, $1,579 to First Presbyterian,

$666 to Fisk University, $555 to Haywood County Memorial Hospital, and $500 to The American Red Cross. His total gross income in 1933 was $65,869.56, of which $22,916.66 was his salary as president of National Life and Accident Insurance Company with the balance coming from interest and dividend income. This meant he gave away nearly 11.7 percent of his gross income that year. While very wealthy, he was not, as many people in Brownsville seemed to think, "the richest man in the country."

On Christmas Eve, Ridley spoke over WSM to National Life's employees. Of course, WSM's radio audience was infinitely larger than that. One of the thousands of listeners was Charles Trabue, president of the Nashville Trust Company. He and Marshall Hotchkiss "dropped in on National Life's Christmas Eve program" on the General Electric radio that Mr. Charles Nelson was giving his son, Charlie, as a Christmas present. Mr. Nelson wrote Ridley on December 27 to say, "It was one of the most impressive radio programs I ever listened to. Your talk was perfect and I think that your feeling and your sense of relationship with your employees is one of the main reasons for the outstanding success of National Life." Nelson went on to congratulate Wills on the company's success that he felt "was largely due to you and your attitude toward the people that make the company." Tom Steele Jr. of Ripley, Tennessee, also heard the program. He wrote to ask if the Barlow knife that Mr. Wills mentioned having received as a Christmas present when he was a small boy was an IXL Wostenholm knife. Ridley wrote him back that he didn't remember, but that if the Wostenholm knife was expensive, it probably was not the kind he received as "my family didn't have much money." A third listener was Bob Weaver, who wrote Wills to say that "it came in fine" in Tupelo.

In 1933, Ridley's total income was $65,869.56. When he filed his federal income tax return in April 1934, his tax was $7,024.87. The same day, W.D. "Uncle Billy" Moore, husband of Mann and Ridley's aunt Eva Moore, was buried in Oakwood Cemetery. Ridley and Jessie were probably among the family members at the funeral. Uncle Billy, who lived to be 91, was later described by Robert Wills Sturdivant as "a dapper, little man who likes to dress up and ride around town in a buggy, but never hit a lick of work." He did manage to get a government pension as a veteran of the Spanish-American War. Because Billy and Eva never had children, Eva always considered Mann and Ridley her surrogate children.

Ridley received one of the most rewarding honors of his life in June 1934 when he was elected to the Board of Trust of Vanderbilt University. Ridley filled the vacancy created when Robert Fenner Jackson, a prominent Nashville attorney, died. In the same meeting, Wills, neither a Vanderbilt alumnus nor even a high school graduate, was elected to serve on the Executive Committee for the 1934-35 school year. He attended his first meeting when the Executive Committee met in the Directors' Room at the American National Bank on August 7. Serving with Wills on the Executive Committee were Andrew Benedict, the university's secretary-treasurer; P.D. Houston, chairman of the board of First American; Robert Cheek, a Nashville financier; and Gerald Henderson, secretary of the Executive Committee. Ridley's first significant contribution to the board came almost immediately when he was named chairman of the Solicitation Committee to raise money for the Vanderbilt Foundation. This nonprofit organization was established January 1, 1935, by friends and alumni of Vanderbilt "for the purpose of making available scholarships, aid and loans to Vanderbilt students, with approved scholarship records, who have shown qualities of leadership in desirable student activities." Two years earlier, Vanderbilt had decided to give 10 scholarships annually to freshmen from outside Nashville. Previous to that, practically all scholarships were available only to upperclassmen. The May 1935 issue of *The Vanderbilt Alumnus* featured a photograph of Wills on its cover. In an editorial, the editor wrote, "This month we honor W.R. Wills, President of the National Life and Accident Insurance Company and member of the Board of Trust of Vanderbilt University, who served as chairman of the Solicitation Committee for securing contributions to the Vanderbilt Foundation. The campaign was a success – a result that is directly attributable to the willing service and unselfish influence of Mr. Wills." In 1935-1936, Ridley was on the board's Executive and Finance committees.

Another way Ridley intended to help Vanderbilt was to establish a psychiatric treatment center at Vanderbilt Hospital. Because of his own serious bouts of depression during the 1920s, Ridley felt it important

110

that people in the Midsouth with psychiatric problems be able to receive help at Vanderbilt and not have to go to the Battle Creek Sanitarium or Johns Hopkins for treatment. As soon as he had time, he intended to follow up on this idea with hospital administrators.

Ridley and Jessie's third grandson and fifth grandchild, William Ridley Wills II, was born June 19, 1934. Before his first birthday, Jessie and Ridley began calling him "Wiggie." On little Ridley's first birthday, Mr. Wills, whom his grandchildren would call "Papa" Wills, wrote his newest grandson a letter, enclosing 10 shares of National Life stock. He said, "This starts you on the road to wealth and I hope you will be economical and less wiggly than you have been thus far." The precedent of giving his grandchildren 10 shares of National Life stock started when Eleanor turned 1, and it would continue for each of his grandchildren.

In 1934, the First Presbyterian Church was headed for a deficit at year-end, as had been the case every year since 1929. That fall, the elders and deacons of the church met to consider the adoption of what was known as the Belmont Covenant Plan of Giving. The idea was to ask all the members, if possible, to "give to the First Presbyterian Church of Nashville one-tenth of our incomes for the period January 1, 1935, and ending March 31, 1935, which shall be in lieu of our present pledges for that period." The 52 church officers endorsed the plan at a buffet supper given by Mr. and Mrs. Wills at their beautiful new home, Far Hills, on October 8, 1934. Wills, one of the leading elders in the church, had been instrumental, in 1925, in having church services broadcast over WSM and, in 1930, arranging for National Life to lend the church $55,000 to enable the church to pay off its pledge to the Presbyterian College of Southwestern and purchase Mrs. John Hill Eakin's home on Hillsboro Pike at an auction sale. In March 1933, when the Session learned that their beloved pastor, James I. Vance, was in failing health, they asked Wills, one of Vance's close friends, to write the aging minister, encouraging him to start his vacation at once and not return to the city until the first of October.

In August 1935, Ridley and Jessie took their son and daughter-in-law, Jesse and Ellen Wills, to Atlantic City for a week's vacation. They stayed at the new 1,000-room, 15-story-tall Chalfont-Haddon Hall Hotel, built by Leeds & Lippencott Co., to replace the late nineteenth century Chafonte and Haddon Hall hotels that stood side by side on the Boardwalk. The new hotel, on the corner of the Boardwalk and North Carolina Avenue, was Atlantic City's largest. While in Atlantic City, both Wills parents and grandparents missed little Matt and Ridley, who were staying at Meade Haven, the Wills' home on Belle Meade Boulevard, with their Buckner grandparents. On August 28, Jesse wrote Master Matt Wills, promising to bring him some toys. The next day, Mrs. Wills, whom the grandchildren would call "Mamma" Wills, wrote Matt to say, "I want to see you and Wiggie so much."

Ridley Wills celebrated his 64th birthday on Thursday, September 19, 1935. That morning, before work, a group of home office girls gathered in Mr. Wills' office to decorate his desk with flowers, fruit and a marvelously designed birthday cake, baked by Nashville's premier cake maker, Mrs. Lavender. The cake, fruit and flowers were a surprise gift from all the home office "girls," given with their sincere wishes for many more happy birthdays.

At a Chamber of Commerce meeting that fall, Pat Mann Estes, legal counsel for Life and Casualty Insurance Company of Tennessee, told his cousin Ridley that he was mailing him a copy of the genealogy of the Mann family. When the package came, Pat's note said, "The genealogy goes no further back than to the grandfather of Joel Mann," as that was as far as the records in Amelia County, Virginia, went. Pat also enclosed a copy of the will of Joel Mann and his wife, Eliza, who were Ridley and Pat's great-grandparents. Pat's mother was the former Martha Ann Mann, daughter of Austin Mann, a son of Joel Mann and a brother of Ridley's grandfather, Asa Mann.

With four young grandchildren, Christmas was special for Ridley and Jessie. As he had done since becoming president in 1931, Ridley spoke to National Life's employees across the country over WSM on Christmas Eve. Although Jessie took care of buying most family presents, Ridley mailed Christmas checks to all the employees at Haywood County Memorial Hospital. The cover of the December 1935 issue of the *Home Office Shield* featured photographs of all the children and grandchildren of the Home Office family. Jessie and Ridley had fun identifying the children, including Eleanor, Matt, Phoebe and Ridley.

Mrs. Wills dearly loved her oldest grandchild, Eleanor. When the

"Our Shield" photograph of Ridley Wills on his 64th birthday.

113

little girl was 5 years old, Mamma Wills gave an elaborate outdoor party for her at Far Hills. A photograph of the party shows a mechanized boat ride in which four little metal boats, each holding three 5-year-olds, go round and round, suspended a few inches off the ground. A teenaged attendant watches over the scene. In another photograph of the same party, which took place in June 1935, baby Ridley is being carried by a black nurse, while another black nurse has little Matt by the hand. Both nurses are wearing starched white uniforms. Seated nearby in metal folding chairs or standing are young mothers in summer dresses and hats, while their children, mostly Eleanor's age, dressed in their party clothes, are sitting or standing on the grass. At one of the parties Mrs. Wills gave for Eleanor, a friend, Everett Kelley, won a white rat. His father must not have been thrilled when Everett brought it home. In 1952, Everett would marry Eleanor.

Despite the Depression, National Life continued to show positive growth in 1935, gaining $17,596,735 in Ordinary life insurance in force that year and $41,234,663 in Industrial growth. The field force in 1935 consisted of 1,305 agents and 324 superintendents, a 59 percent

Birthday party for Eleanor Craig, age 5, at Far Hills. Phoebe Clark is in the boat on the extreme left while her first cousin, Matt Buckner Wills, is in the boat immediately in front of the ride operator.

114

reduction from 1934. When agents or superintendents quit, as many did in the tough Depression years, National Life simply did not replace them. The wife of an agent with another debit company, who owed Mr. Wills $25, wrote him to say that her husband "couldn't sell insurance when people were starving but that we will repay the debt as soon as we can."

Among the things Jessie and Ridley Wills were thankful for at Christmas 1935 were the continuance of Ridley's good health, their four healthy grandchildren and the wonderful reputation their son, Jesse, had made for himself. He was a deacon at the First Presbyterian Church and, since 1934, had been assistant manager of the Ordinary Department and a vice-president at National Life. Jesse was having great success in hybridizing iris in the lot behind Meade Haven. When the American Iris Society met in Nashville the previous April, Jesse impressed the AIS president Dr. Harry Everett and other national leaders. Soon, they would ask him to judge a regional iris show. In 1943, Jesse would be elected president of the American Iris Society. In 1947, he would be awarded the Dykes Medal, the highest award given by the American Iris Society, for his blue bearded iris, Chivalry, that he hybridized in 1943.

Chapter X

1936 — The Saddest Year

January started on a deceptively positive note. On the first day of the year, Ridley took possession of a 139-acre farm in the 14th Civil District of Williamson County on the old Harvey Turnpike Road. He bought the farm, which included a farmhouse suitable for a tenant farmer, for $8,700 from the heirs of John C. Seward. Ridley envisioned the farm as a nearby place to go to on weekends to escape the stress of work. He also planned to have horses there for his grandchildren to ride when they were older. With a farm, four grandchildren, and with National Life continuing to do well despite the Depression, Ridley had reason to be euphoric.

During January, Ridley received the usual number of personal requests for help. Henry Berry of Jackson, Tennessee, wanted Wills to help him collect a loan. Mrs. J.M. Dowdie of Memphis begged him to help her husband get a WPA job with the City of Memphis. She had a family of five and didn't have the money to pay her rent for February. Ridley couldn't help Mr. Berry, but he did write the WPA director in Memphis in an effort to get Mr. Dowdie a job. None were available.

He also wrote Lewis Burnett, regional manager of Home Owners Loan Corporation in Memphis about "a young man in your organization whose mother and father here in Nashville are close friends of mine." Wills said: "Although I don't know the young man personally, it is my belief that he is worthwhile in every way. Anything that can be done toward his advancement will be greatly appreciated by a great many people in Nashville who have the highest possible regard for Mr. and Mrs. Alexander, Sr."

Early in February, Harvey C. Alexander Jr. wrote Wills from Memphis to say that he appreciated Wills' letter to Mr. Burnett but that "I was very sorry to read that you did not know me since I can hardly remember when I did not know you. Had I thought you would not remember me, I would never have had my mother ask you for the letter. It caused her no little embarrassment."

W.J. "Bill" Anderson, executive of the Nashville Council of the Boy

Scouts of America, wrote Wills to advise him that he had been elected a member of the Nashville Council. He asked Ridley to attend the annual meeting on January 29, on the fifth floor of the Chamber of Commerce building. Already serving on the Vanderbilt and Monroe Harding Children's Home boards, having just stepped down as an adviser to the Junior League of Nashville, serving as an active ruling elder at First Presbyterian Church and having just agreed to accept a three-year term on the Community Chest Board, Ridley wrote Anderson that he could not accept the position because "I have as many of these things as I can possibly give attention to, and to just use my name without my doing anything is not appealing to me. In addition to this, you have Mr. CA. Craig of our organization on your council."[62] Ridley made one more point, "I assume you know that I am greatly interested in the work of the Boy Scouts and have undertaken to help them in a material way."

Of all the requests Ridley received in the 1930s, the one that may have touched him the most came early in 1936 from a younger Brownsville friend, Dr. John Thornton Sr., who, when he wrote Ridley was on the staff of Haywood County Memorial Hospital. Thornton asked Wills' help in getting his son, John, then a student at Vanderbilt, some sort of scholarship. Ridley immediately wrote Dr. W.S. Leathers, dean of the Vanderbilt Medical School, to ask for financial aid for the younger Thornton. He told the dean that John "is finishing this year in the Literary Department and is making a good record." Wills spoke of John's solid family and background and said, "I have seen him frequently since he has been at Vanderbilt."

In a letter to Wills written a few days later, Thornton Sr. spoke more directly to his son's need for financial aid. He said, "As you probably know, I own no property having lost my farm during the Depression and am entirely dependent on my practice to continue John in school. The early frost got the doctor's cotton last fall, and unless I can make some other arrangements, I fear it will be necessary to take John out of school next year. Both he and I would greatly appreciate anything that you could do toward obtaining a scholarship for him." A week later,

---

62   Mr. C. A. Craig became the first of four generations of his family to service on the Nashville Council of Boy Scouts of America.

Ridley wrote Leathers again. To strengthen his case, he enclosed a copy of Thornton's second letter.

With the help of a scholarship and possibly financial assistance from Wills, John Thornton Jr. went on to Vanderbilt Medical School, graduating in 1940. He completed his internship at the Butterworth Hospital in Grand Rapids, Michigan, before serving as a physician in the U.S. Army from 1941 until 1946. After the war, he returned to Brownsville to practice and rear a family of four children. When he retired in 1986, he was honored with a reception at which someone said, "Dr. Thornton Jr. has maintained his medical practice in Brownsville for the past 40 years. During this time, he delivered many of the people in this room, cared for us when we were sick, and shared with us, both day and night, some of our happiest moments of joy, and our saddest moments of grief. We have seen many changes in the world over the past 40 years, but one of the things that has remained constant in Brownsville over those years is that Dr. Thornton has always been available to serve the needs of his patients." Ridley Wills would never know what a critical role he played in shaping John Thornton Jr.'s life.

W. Frederick Williams Jr., a stockbroker with Burton, Cluett & Dana in New York City's financial district and who was married to the former Margaret Nelson of Atlanta, Jessie's niece, approached Wills in February, asking if he might "have a try" at securing some securities for Wills' personal account.[63] Williams had learned that Wills was doing business with The Bank of New York and Trust Co. Wills responded to Fred, advising him "the matter of purchasing bonds for my trusts in New York is in the hands of the bank there." He elaborated: "They do not purchase bonds without my approval and I am inclined to buy Southern tax-free bonds. Because of this, I have found that local dealers have an advantage over New York dealers." Finally, Wills offered to send Fred National Life's schedule of company-owned bonds.

Early in 1936, the bursar's position at Vanderbilt was open. As a member of the Executive Committee that would make the appointment, Ridley got three requests to support Tom LeSueur for the post. John

---

63 Margaret and W. Frederick Williams had three children – W. Frederick Williams III, Margaret Williams and Mildred "Millie" Williams.

Sloan, president of the Nashville Vanderbilt Club, solicited Ridley's help for Tom, who was married to a first cousin of Ridley's daughter-in-law, Ellen Buckner Wills. Someone else wanted Ridley to support Will Howard, a former Founder's Medalist at Vanderbilt, for the position. Wills said he would support Tom LeSueur "if the opportunity presented itself."

A cousin of Ridley's, Mrs. Brooks Crawford, of Brownsville, was the Haywood County representative of the Tennessee Emergency Relief Administration in 1935 and 1936. Concerned that there was an effort to replace her, she turned to Ridley. He wrote Gov. Hill McAlister that he understood there was interest in replacing Crawford and that he would like to meet with the governor before any action was taken. In his letter, Wills praised her performance and added, "I am as much devoted to Haywood County and its people as could be possible." McAlister wrote Ridley, "There will be no interference with the lady."

A different kind of request came a few days later in March. R.P. Berry, a representative of the Louisville and Nashville Railroad in Brownsville, wrote Wills to say that the house he was renting from National Life for $20 a month was not in a livable condition and did not even have a water connection. He said he hated to move because he had just planted a spring garden but would have to if something was not done. Wills responded with a letter in which he said he "mistakenly thought everything had been fixed up" and that Robert Sturdivant, who handled mortgage loans for National Life in West Tennessee, "would be in town the following Tuesday to set thing right."[64] Wills said he was "interested in your case on account of your kindness to my aunt (Mrs. Eva Mann Moore)."

Ridley traveled to New Orleans and Florida on business early in 1936. Jessie was, by then, accustomed to being in her big house alone because Ridley was often on the road. Glad to be home, he took time to read, the first week in April, the annual statement of First Presbyterian Church. He noted, with satisfaction that the church had paid off a $2,724.71 loan

---

64   Bob and Trousdale Wills Sturdivant moved to Nashville in 1929 where they lived at 1303 Ashwood Ave. They later moved to Richland Avenue. Mr. Sturdivant was a graduate of Webb School, where he learned Greek and Latin so well that he could read both languages all his life.

to National Life. A week later, the church treasurer, Joe Vaulx Crockett, sent Wills a copy of the Eakin Committee statement, saying "I don't know that you have any business with it, except that your position as coadjutor to Bishop White may entitle you to almost anything." The Eakin Committee, consisting of the eldest elders in length of service, was responsible for administering the John Hill Eakin Fund. "Bishop White" was likely a reference to David Walker White, who had been a ruling elder at First Presbyterian since 1919.

Things began to unravel in April 1936. On April 20, after returning from a tiring two-week trip, Ridley wrote Mann, concerned about hearing that Macon Thornton "has not been doing well and was taken to Mayo's Clinic." He also told Mann that he would be happy to lend him some money whenever he needed it. On May 1, Mann responded by letter, thanking Ridley for the offer, saying that, "by stinting and living economically, I don't need it just now but might call on you later in the summer." He added, "You have been mighty good to me. Today is my 66th birthday and [I am] feeling fairly well." Mann went on to report that his brother-in-law, Macon, "stood the trip to Mayo Clinic all right" but he doubted if he "would find relief." Macon's wife, Fannie, and brother, Harbert Thornton, who paid for the trip, had persuaded him to go.

In May, Ridley went to Philadelphia where he hosted a luncheon for Philadelphia field men at the Ben Franklin Hotel. He also kept abreast of negotiations with two companies on the purchase of an air-conditioning unit for the Haywood County Memorial Hospital. When the hospital trustees accepted a bid of $920 from the Southern Supply Company of Jackson, Wills paid the invoice.

On the evening of Wednesday, May 13, Ridley drove to the office and spoke on an "Insurance Week" program at WSM. W.D. "Will" Trabue, a friend of Wills, heard his remarks. The next day, Will wrote Ridley to say that he had listened to the program. He said he did so not because he had a keen interest in "Insurance Week" but because he hoped Ridley would give some sage advice outside of insurance. He said "I was somewhat disappointed when you did not. I think," Trabue wrote, "a man of your standing, when he has access to the radio, ought to tell the balance of us what to expect of our government and how to arrange our own lives and finances in a manner to make the best of the situation." Later that week, Charles E. Diehl, the president of Southwestern College called on Wills at his office. Although Wills was out, he saw Jesse and later wrote Wills inviting him to attend the Southwestern commencement the following week and, if that was inconvenient, he asked if he might see him on June 4. Batsell Baxter, president of David Lipscomb College, also contacted Wills that spring. He wrote to thank him for his $250 payment on his pledge to the school. Baxter said Wills' and other's expressions of confidence offset "all the hardships and sacrifices connected with the work."

Ridley got a phone call on June 14, 1936, that stunned him. Della told him that his brother, Mann, had committed suicide earlier that day. She said when she could not get Mann to respond after he had been in the bathroom a long time, she tried to open the door only to find it was locked from the inside. That week, their grandsons, Herbert and Wills Oglesby, then 16 and 10 years old, respectively, happened to be staying with them while their parents, Harriette and Herbert Oglesby, were on vacation in the Pacific Northwest. Herbert put a ladder up to the bathroom window and climbed in. He discovered his grandfather lying motionless in the bathtub. Della called a neighbor, George Reid, who came over and quickly realized that Mann was dead. He called Dr. T. Crowder Chapman, the Haywood County coroner. Chapman immediately came to the Wills residence on Park Street and officially pronounced Mann Wills dead.[65]

The *Jackson Sun* published an editorial on Mann Wills "who died Sunday." That week, Della received letters of condolence from all over the country. She also received telegrams, as well as food and delicacies that filled her icebox and covered the kitchen and dining room tables. Scores of people in Brownsville and vicinity called or came by. These expressions of sorrow helped sustain her during this nightmarish ordeal. At the funeral, a large number of former members of his Sunday School class were on hand to pay their respects. Mann had taught the class for 30 years. He also had served First Presbyterian Church as a deacon, ordained in 1901; as assistant superintendent of the Sunday Schools in

---

65   During the 1980s, Dr. Chapman, a Vanderbilt graduate and former mayor of Brownsville, told Pat Mann, Jr. the circumstances of Mr. Wills' death.

1910; and as a ruling elder. John Mann, a planter and cotton ginner in Marianna, Arkansas, wrote Ridley to express his sorrow over Mann's death. John said, "I always felt like he and Papa were pretty much of the same type and I know he will be missed around Brownsville as well as by the family." Before Ridley left Brownsville after the funeral, he promised to help Della all he could.

A few days later, Brownsville attorney, John T. Gray Jr., a fellow elder with Mann at the First Presbyterian Church and the executor of Mann's estate, drove up to Nashville to discuss estate issues with Ridley. The same day, Ridley wrote Della that Mann had taken out a $1,000 life insurance policy with National Life in 1921 with him as beneficiary because "of what Mann owed me." Ridley enclosed the company's check for $731.61 that he endorsed over to her. He explained that Mann had borrowed $225 on the policy. He went on to say that Mann had other policies with the company on which she was the beneficiary and that the Death Claims Department would handle them directly with her. Ridley told Della he did not see any reason to come back to Brownsville then but would "await developments." Although Ridley did not mention it in his letter, Della had told him when he was in Brownsville for the funeral that Mann had been increasingly depressed over his financial problems, and those of his son.

In response to Ridley's letter, Della wrote thanking him for giving her the life insurance proceeds and asking him to invest it for her. She spoke movingly of her brother-in-law's kind and loving support, saying that, for the past three years, she had tried "to show my poor darling that he was all that amounted to anything to me in the whole wide world, but I couldn't and didn't help him. You did all in your power to help him but he was so sick that neither of us could reach him."

Della said she had many questions and then addressed some of those she felt needed immediate attention. She spoke of how expensive it was to keep up her house, including paying the cook, who also did the laundry ($2.50 a week), and the hired black man, John, who milked the two cows, kept up the place and tilled the garden ($4 a week). She mentioned that John also had free board. She asked Ridley if she should let one go. She said her daughter, Elizabeth, hoped to take her to the mountains for a little rest but that they could not go then because Elizabeth was helping John Gray Jr. deal with estate matters. Della also reflected on what a wonderful friend John had been over the years. Later, Della sold her house, discharged the servants and moved to Memphis where she would live with her unmarried daughter, Elizabeth, until her own death in 1953.

In the summer, Wills visited the National Life office in Columbus, Georgia. While there, he made an appointment to see the commanding officer at the Infantry School at Fort Benning. There, Wills asked that National Life agents be allowed on the base to sell policies and collect premiums. Soon, Col. F.G. Kellond, acting commandant of the Infantry School, wrote Wills to say that he could find no record of National Life having made application for a permit to sell insurance on the base, but that, upon receipt of such an application, "it will be given every consideration."

Two National Life events of significance took place in the summer of 1936. The company celebrated its 35th anniversary. The company founders and senior officers were all there. They included C.A. Craig, chairman of the board; Ridley Wills, president; C.R. Clements, executive vice-president; Dr. Rufus E. Fort, vice-president and medical director; and Thomas J. Tyne, vice-president and general counsel.

The other event was the establishment of a picnic for the company's colored employees. Wills was undoubtedly instrumental in this happening. It was held at Hopkins Park, 10.5 miles from Nashville on Nolensville Pike. There, the colored employees and their families could play croquet, baseball or tennis. Others could pitch horseshoes with their children or grandchildren. There was a cold-drink stand and plenty of food.

The last week in July, Macon Thornton died in Brownsville. Ridley and Jessie went down for the funeral at Tabernacle Methodist Church. There, Della remembered Ridley telling her that he and Jessie were going to Europe in August but that, when they got back, he would come back to Brownsville and "make ample provision for my future." She also recalled that he said, "I want you to be secure for life. Mann was all that I had left and I want to help you."

A few weeks earlier, Ridley had written his friend, Cordell Hull, secretary of state, informing him that he and Mrs. Wills were making their first trip to Europe and would appreciate any introductions he could make for them with American embassies in London, Edinburgh, Paris and possibly other major European cities. On July 17, Hull wrote a letter to the American Diplomatic and Consular Officers taking pleasure in introducing W.R. Wills of Nashville and his wife and asking them to extend whatever courtesies and assistance "as you may be able to render."

In August, Mr. and Mrs. Ridley Wills and Mr. and Mrs. Thomas J. Tyne sailed from New York to Europe on the *S.S. Manhattan*, "the world's newest luxury liner." The trip had been planned for them by Virginia Matthews of the Bourne Travel Agency, located in the lobby of the Nashville Trust Company at

Off for Six Weeks' European Tour

MR. AND MRS. W. RIDLEY WILLS are seen aboard the S.S. Manhattan just before they sailed Wednesday from New York for a six weeks' European tour which will include visits to Scotland, England and France. They will return to the United States on the S.S. Queen Mary.

Mr. and Mrs. Ridley Wills on the S.S. Manhattan, New York Harbor, August 1936.

315 Union St. The Wills, on their first trip to Europe, were gone six weeks, during which they visited Scotland, England and France. Ridley's son, Jesse, remembered that, shortly before his parents left, his father was in unusually high spirits and more talkative than usual. On the 15th, Mrs. Wills wrote Jesse that they were having "a lovely trip, smooth seas, no one sick and lots of nice people." She also praised the food and added how much she missed the children. In London, she fired off postcards to each of her grandchildren. In one to Matt, she said she thought of "you, Eleanor, Phoebe and Wiggs so much." Two days later, she sent Matt a postcard of the Royal Horse Guards Whitehall that she had seen. The Wills returned to New York in September on the *S.S. Queen Mary*. The reached home in time to be on hand on the 25th when Ellen delivered a healthy baby girl, whom she and Jesse named Ellen McClung Wills for her mother.

Four days earlier, on September 21, Ridley got more good news. The *Wall Street Journal* ran a favorable story on National Life, identifying the company as one of the biggest bond buyers in the South. It said the company's bond account "now exceeds $24 million." The article pointed out that the company's five founders, all still active as officers and directors, "have seen National Life and Accident expand from an institution with only a few thousand dollars of assets to a place with total assets of approximately $45,000,000." The article went on to speak of the company's "own big edifice on top of a hill overlooking Nashville's business district" and of the company's radio station WSM with its 878-foot tower, "the tallest radio tower in America," and mentioned the sound of the Pan American being broadcast every day into nearly every state in the union from a remote transmitter 12 miles south of town.

On September 28, Will T. Cheek, chairman of the Airport Committee, appointed Wills as a member of the Reception and Entertainment Committee for the dedication of Nashville's new airport on November 1.

The only sad news was that, during September, Ridley and his fellow members of the Session of the First Presbyterian Church reluctantly accepted the resignation of Dr. James I. Vance, whose failing health had not improved. The elders named a nomination committee, chaired by Wills, to recommend a successor. In October, the nomination committee announced it was ready to report and called a congregational meeting for that purpose. At the meeting, Wills read the report. He began by outlining the committee's reasons for suggesting Dr. Thomas C. Barr as Vance's successor. Wills said that Barr "had been tried as an assistant pastor for seven years and was well known and loved by the congregation." He then nominated Barr as pastor of the church to succeed Vance, "recently resigned and now pastor emeritus of the church." After several motions were made, but failed, to delay the action, Professor Clarence Wallace read a letter from Vance, dated October 22, 1936, that said, "The duty of every member of the First Church is to foster the spirit of harmonious action and Dr. Barr through a long and critical period has shown that he can lead the church that way." In the ensuing vote by ballot, Reverend Thomas C. Barr received 535 votes. Seventy-eight members voted against electing him, and one ballot was marked "uncertain." The Presbytery approved the action the following month and, on November 29, 1936, Barr was installed. The ailing Vance made a special effort to come to Nashville for the installation.

Woodall Rodgers, a partner in Turner, Rodgers and Winn, in Dallas, an alumni representative on the Vanderbilt Board of Trust; and the university's most prominent alumnus in Texas, learned, in September, that fellow Vanderbilt trustee Ridley Wills was coming to Dallas on October 14 for an American Life Convention. He wrote Ridley on October 6 to invite him to attend the Vanderbilt Alumni Association reunion in Dallas on October 16. That evening, Rodgers wrote, there would be a special performance of the "Cavalcade" at the Texas Centennial Exposition. He also offered to get Wills tickets to the Vanderbilt-SMU game the next day. Rodgers said that Chancellor and Mrs. Kirkland would be there. At the bottom of his letter, Rodgers wrote, "Don't Miss It Young Fellow!"

Ridley Wills responded to Rogers' letter on October 8, saying "I will be in Dallas from Wednesday [the 14th] to Friday attending the American Life Convention." Having been told about the Vanderbilt-SMU game on Saturday, Wills wrote, "I have decided to stay over for this game. I already have my football ticket, my hotel reservation in Dallas and my Pullman for the return from Dallas. I am not an alumnus of Vanderbilt and do not think I have any right to participate in the activities of the Alumni Association. It is a sad confession, but I really am an uneducated man. If you can help me into any of those fine affairs without exposing me I will take a chance and it will be appreciated. The young fellow who is writing this letter is only sixty-five years old and is trying to not miss very much of what is going on in the world today."

The day before leaving Nashville with his son, Jesse, and other National Life officials, Ridley wrote Della that he was leaving for Dallas and that it probably would be two or three weeks before he could come to Brownsville to see her. If he got tied up, he said it might be necessary for her to come to see him in Nashville. Another reason the National Life officials were going to Dallas was to see National Life's exhibit at the Texas Centennial. The name of the exhibit was "The Texas-Tennessee Hall of Heroes.

While attending the American Life Convention in Dallas with his father, Jesse Wills realized that Wills was in an abnormally euphoric mood. Jesse became seriously concerned that "this period of elation would be followed by a period of depression such as he had suffered from previously." Instead, shortly after the Texas trip, Ridley Wills had a complete breakdown. "Everything snapped suddenly," Jesse recalled in a December 3, 1948, letter to Della. Following this, Jesse started looking after his father's affairs under an informal agreement between his mother, his sister, himself and his father's bank. Jesse didn't think it was necessary or advisable to do anything more "because the doctors all assured us that dad would recover. I carried on more or less like he had. I continued his charitable contributions and I was able to do such things as help Virginia finish at Vanderbilt and help support Ridley's children when his affairs got to a crisis."[66] He said he did not know that his father had been giving Mann checks on "regular intervals monthly" but rather thought "they were larger checks and at less frequent intervals, but they may have been both."

National Life took another hit when founder, Thomas J. Tyne, died of a heart attack on November 1, 1936. He had complained of not feeling well on his recent trip with Ridley and Jessie to Europe. With Tom Tyne dead, and two more founders and executive officers, Runcie Clements and Ridley Wills, in hospitals, Mr. Craig realized he needed to conserve his strength and pass on company responsibility to younger officials. By the second week in December, Mr. Clements, who had surgery, was convalescing and expected to be back in the office early in January. The news about Wills was unsettling. He had not improved. Despite this, Mrs. Wills and Jesse felt comfortable that Wills' nurse, Paul Rebman, was doing a conscientious and professional job. Both Dr. Al Harris, the physician in charge of Wills, and Dr. Frank W. Stephens, the director of City View Sanitarium, "were absolutely confident that a recovery of some sort would take place in a year to eighteen months."

---

66   Virginia Sturdivant was a member of Kappa Alpha Theta at Vanderbilt. She married Harlan Dodson June 28, 1941.

CHAPTER XI

National Life held its 35-year anniversary celebration in the home office in February 1937. As part of the program, oil portraits of the five founders were commissioned and placed in the Directors' Room. President Ridley Wills was, of course, ill and unable to be present. Not only was Wills not there, he was unaware of the event.

Three months later, Wills did not take it in that his great nephew, Robert Wills Sturdivant, graduated from Vanderbilt Law School as the Founder's Medalist, recognizing his status as the No. 1 student in his law school class, despite having to work at night at WSM to pay his way through law school. There, as an announcer on WSM FM, Bob got to know the staff, artists and composers who appreciated him for his wit and intelligence. When he left WSM upon graduation, his first cousin, Herbert Wills Oglesby, then a sophomore at Vanderbilt, took his place. At the time of his graduation, Bob's grade point average in law school was higher than that of any other VU Law School graduate in history. How proud Mann Wills would have been.

Bob went on to be one of Nashville's finest attorneys at Trabue and Sturdivant, a firm he and Charles C. Trabue founded. The firm later became Trabue, Sturdivant, and DeWitt. Bob was happily married to the former Elizabeth Nininger for 41 years. They had three sons, Robert Wills Sturdivant Jr., Charles Nininger Sturdivant

Christ Church Episcopal Mardi Gras Celebration, February 9, 1937, Belmont Theater. Pictured left to right: Phoebe Clark, Lady of the Court; Ridley Wills II, Lord of the Court; Eleanor Clark, Queen Elizabeth; and Matt B. Wills, Lord of the Court.

and Thomas English Sturdivant, and five grandchildren.

Ridley Wills' real estate and cash assets were valued, in August 1937, at $158,836, of which the 15.44 acres on Curtiswood Lane represented the largest component. Wills' second largest asset, excluding stocks and bonds, was cash of $45,805.10. Of this, $10,967.90 was in Third National Bank. The balance was in the Bank of New York. The second-largest real estate-related asset consisted of notes totaling $18,180 that represented loans Wills made to Jesse to enable him to buy his house on Belle Meade Boulevard. Wills lent his son this money "for the purpose of preserving an equity in my estate as between my son,

Ellen and Jesse Wills, standing behind their sones, Ridley and Matt with their daughter, Ellen, sitting on a wooden rooster. Far Hills, Christmas, 1937.

Jesse, and my daughter, Mamie Craig." Ridley's 139-acre farm in the 14th Civil District of Williamson County, valued at $10,000, was his third-largest real estate asset.[67] The Women's Club of Nashville still owed him $7,381.50 in principal and interest for his old residence at 217 Louise Ave. He also owned two lots on Linden Avenue, valued at $2,000, and half interest in the lot on the corner of State Street and Louise Avenue that he and Runcie Clements bought when their children were young as a place for the neighborhood children to play. Ridley's interest was appraised at $500.

Six months after Wills' breakdown, there were no signs of improvement. With his father's federal income tax due, Jesse Wills filed

---

67 Mr. Wills had earlier sold the 300-acre farm in Haywood County's 8th Civil District that had been left jointly to him and Mann when their mother died in 1907. As part of the real estate settlement after her death, Ridley bought his brother's 50 percent interest in the farm and sold Mann his interest in her other Haywood County properties.

the return with the following sworn statement: "I, Jesse E. Wills, swear that I am the son and agent of W.R. Wills, that W.R. Wills, for the past year, has been confined to a sanitarium and will be so confined, according to his attending physicians' opinions, probably for an additional period of six months or longer; that because of such necessary confinement and illness he is unable to make and swear to this return or to execute a power of attorney authorizing me to do so.

I further swear that this return (including its accompanying schedules and statements, if any) has been examined by me, and to the best of my knowledge and belief is a true, correct and complete return made for said W.R. Wills for the taxable year stated, pursuant to the Revenue Act of 1936 and the regulations issued there under."

Entrance from Rose Garden to Formal Garden, Far Hills, 1936.

In the winter of 1938, the Women's Division of West End United Methodist Church asked Mrs. Wills if she would open her garden for the spring pilgrimage as she had done in 1937, Mrs. Wills, who spent time in her rose garden every morning during the spring months, agreed to do so and the Far Hills Garden was on the April tour. [68]

Jesse naturally kept Mr. Craig and Mr. Clements informed as to his father's condition. With the prospects dim for Wills' return to National Life in the foreseeable future, the company's board, in 1938, granted Wills a leave of absence, created a new position of vice-chairman of the board, and elected him

68   The April 1947 spring tour of noted gardens was publicized in a story in the Nashville Banner on April 2. That story featured a photograph of the five oldest Wills grandchildren – Eleanor Clark, Matt Wills, Phoebe Clark, Ridley Wills II and Ellen Wills – playing near the reflecting pool at Far Hills.

to that post. Runcie Clements succeeded Ridley as president, while Craig continued as chairman of the board. By this time, Jesse had requested all the other boards that Wills served on to accept his resignation due to ill health. This included the Vanderbilt Board.

In June, the Vanderbilt Alumni Magazine featured a photograph of Sam H. Mann Jr., L'14, St. Petersburg, Fla. Attorney, vice president of the [Vanderbilt] Alumni Association for the Southern area. Jesse saw the picture of his cousin and reflected on how much things had changed since his father's picture graced the cover of the same magazine three years earlier.

Mrs. Wills, who had held up remarkably well since her husband's mental collapse, needed to get away. In July 1939, she took Mamie Craig and her two daughters, Eleanor and Phoebe, to the Chalfonte-Haddon Hall Hotel in Atlantic City. Her newest grandchild, George Wills Clark, born March 12, 1937, stayed home with a nurse. Mrs. Wills was back home before Jesse and Ellen left on a trip to Eastern Canada. On August 19, she wrote them in care of the Chateau Frontenac in Quebec City. Mama Wills said, "I took Matt and Ridley to see The Wizard of Oz yesterday afternoon. I can't say they were thrilled as it scared both of them. Ridley was ready to leave very soon after it started and Matt got on the floor and hid his eyes. He didn't cry or ask to leave but said 'The witch was more scary than the one in Snow White and, if he went again, he would be afraid'" Despite that, Mrs. Wills reported that Matt, Ridley and Ellen were all well and would be at Far Hills for Sunday dinner. The children's other grandparents, Dr. and Mrs. Matt Buckner, had moved to Meade Haven to look after the children while their parents were gone.

Because their house on Craighead was small, Eleanor and Phoebe enjoyed going to their grandmother Wills' spacious house on weekends. They loved playing hide and go seek there. A favorite hiding place for Eleanor was Mamma Wills four-poster bed with heavy curtains on three sides. Maybe the Clark grandchildren were at Far Hills when Ted and Mamie Craig went with Celeste and Walker Casey to attend the black-tie Nashville premier of Gone With the Wind at Loew's Vendome Theater. Some of Ted's friends undoubtedly commented on his likeness to Clark Gable. Both were handsome, fastidious dressers, had mustaches, parted their hair down the middle and often wore white handkerchiefs in their left breast pockets.

Two months before leaving for Canada, Jesse Wills had been named manager of the Ordinary Department at National Life. He was clearly destined to be successful following in his father's footsteps. It was just as clear that, because he felt his father's single-minded devotion to National Life contributed to his breakdown, Jesse would also pursue other interests, such as bird-watching, hybridizing iris, becoming a director of the American Iris Society in 1939 and contributing papers to the Old Oak Literary Club, which he had belonged to since 1929. He also was becoming, as his father had been, a force at First Presbyterian Church, where he was a deacon.

Each year, Jesse, acting for his father, made charitable gifts in Wills' name. In 1940, those gifts totaled $6,591.50, with the two largest going to the Nashville Community Chest ($3,000) and First Presbyterian Church ($2,631.50).

He also reached an agreement with Mrs. J. Hugh Knox, president of the Woman's Club of Nashville, regarding the club's indebtedness to Wills incurred when they purchased his home at 217 Louise Ave. in 1931. Jesse and Knox agreed that the total amount of principal and interest owed to Wills would be reduced to $7,500 and that this amount would be paid in monthly payments at the rate of four percent interest until the indebtedness was retired in 15 years. Knox expressed sincere appreciation to Jesse for his kind consideration in reducing the debt and rate of interest and extending the payment period over a longer period of time.

In 1940, Mamie Craig and Ted Clark commissioned Emmons H. Woolwine and John Harwood, prominent Nashville architects, to design a spacious house for them on the five acres her parents had given her on Curtiswood Lane next to Far Hills. The first floor of the elegant 14-room house, completed in 1941, included an entrance hall with a curved stairway leading to the second floor. To the left on that level were the dining room, kitchen and garage. To the right were a guest bedroom, bathroom, den, small kitchen and a large recreation room that measured 15 feet by 24 feet. Upstairs were four bedrooms and four bathrooms on the south end, an 18-foot-by-24-foot living room in the center, and, beyond it, storage areas over the garage. The living room opened to a balcony with a fine view over the countryside to the west. The house was featured in the May 1941 issue of Nashville's Architectural Record. Once the Clarks moved in, the children spend a great deal of time next door at Far Hills.

Jesse Wills, on behalf of his father, submitted form 1940, on April 15, 1941, to pay Wills'1940 federal income taxes. His total income for 1940 was $67,356.72, of which $66,479.84 represented stock dividends from National Life. Mr. Wills had no salary income from National Life, as his leave of absence had expired. He owed federal income and World War II defense taxes of $18,643.35. Jesse Wills listed rental income of $929.84 from three properties his father owned – a brick store at Eighth and Commerce, acquired in 1925; the farm in Williamson County; and the house on Craighead Avenue he acquired in 1929 for Mamie Craig.

Just as Jessie Ely predicted in 1898, her oldest sister, Miss Mary Mitchell "Mamie" Ely, never married. She died March 13, 1943, at age 76,

Christmas card from Craig and Ted Clark, also showing Eleanor, Phoebe and George, 1940.

HOUSE FOR MR. AND MRS. C. P. CLARK, NASHVILLE, TENN.: EMMONS H. WOOLWINE and JOHN HARWOOD, Architects

HOUSES

This month's group of houses, selected from widely separated regions of this country, vary in size (one to six bedrooms), style, and solution. The basic planning ideas have widespread potential application and adaptability to the fundamental problems of residential planning in any part of the country. As is pointed out many elements conform to the standards mentioned in "How Safe Is The House?" (p. 67).

Home of Mr. and Mrs. C. P. Clark, Architectual Record, May 1941

at the Bedford County Hospital in her hometown of Shelbyville, where she had made her home since moving back from Nashville in the early 1930s. A member of First Presbyterian Church in Nashville, she was survived by two sisters, Jessie Ely Wills and Charlotte Ely (Mrs. Henry) Nelson, of Atlanta.[69] Miss Ely was buried in the Whiteside lot at Willow Mount Cemetery.[70] In the years following Mamie's death, Mrs. Wills would regularly have her chauffeur, Lemmie "Lem" Wilson, drive her to Shelbyville so she could put flowers on the Whiteside lot where her parents, Whiteside grandparents and two sisters, Mamie and Nellie, were buried. Nellie Thompson had died August 8, 1927.[71] Often, Mrs. Wills would be accompanied by her friend, Margaret Lipscomb Thompson, who was also kin to the Whitesides. Margaret and her husband, Overton Thompson, lived at Glen Leven, only a mile or so from Far Hills.

Jesse Wills did not serve in World War II, as he was 42 years old with four dependents when the United States was attacked by the Japanese on December 7, 1941. That Sunday, Mrs. Jessie Wills and the Wills and Clark families had gone to First Presbyterian Church and were at Far Hills for Sunday dinner. The entire family heard the announcement on the radio while in the family sitting room. Sensing the electricity in the sitting room, Matt and Ridley left the toys they were playing with in the toy closet and joined the rest of the family huddled around the radio. The grandchildren heard Ted Clark, who was in the Naval Reserve, excitedly say that he had to get his boat that was docked on the Cumberland River.

Two days before Pearl Harbor, Ridley Wills' great nephew, Herbert Wills Oglesby, dropped out of Vanderbilt to join the Army Air Corps. He took basic training and further training that qualified him as a B-24 pilot. Herbert flew 99 bombing missions over China with Claire Chenault's Flying Tigers.[72] Shot down, he parachuted to safety as natives helped him

---

69   Charlotte Ely (Mrs. Henry) Nelson died in 1960.

70   *The Nashville Tennessean*, May 16, 1943.

71   Nellie's husband T. Leigh Thompson's name is on a marker in Willow Mount, along with Nellie's. His date of death is not on the marker because he was buried in Lone Oak Cemetery in Lewisburg following his death in 1953.

72   Oglesby was awarded the Order of the Clouds and the Chinese Air Hero Medal from the Republic of China.

get back to his Chinese base. Herbert wrote his parents about the ordeal so that they would know what happened and that he was safe. Later, Mr. and Mrs. Oglesby received a letter from the War Department informing them that their son was missing in action.

Herbert Wills Oglesby made the newly formed Air Corps his career after the war ended, attaining the rank of colonel at age 35. He married Lucie Jean Brown in 1943, had two children, Thomas Warren Oglesby and Della Katherine Oglesby McCary, and earned a Ph.D. when he was 71 years old. Herbert died February 10, 1999, and was buried at Arlington National Military Cemetery with full military honors.

Wanting to do something to help the war effort, Herbert's parents, Harriette and Herbert Exum Oglesby, and younger son, Wills Oglesby, moved to Mobile, Alabama, where, with the help of the Isaac B. Tigrett family in Jackson, he got a job with a Tigrett-owned company that was converting yachts to sea-going patrol boats mounted with 20-millimeter machine guns and depth charges. Wills graduated from Mobile's Murphy High School and qualified for the Navy's V-5 pilot training program that required two years of college. To meet that educational requirement, he attended the University of the South for two years. By then the war was over, so Wills transferred to Georgia Tech as an NROTC student. There, his first cousin, William R. "Bill" Wills III, who was also attending Georgia Tech, helped him with his English class. Wills graduated in 1948 and did not have to serve active duty, but he remained in the Naval Reserves for five years. On August 1, 1948, he joined General Shoe Corporation in Nashville where he became a career employee and officer.

Mamie Craig wanted to do her share to help the war effort. She hit upon the idea of having a USO party on her terrace and backyard for U.S. Army Air Corps troops at the Classification Center. Eleanor remembers the party well because it was the first occasion she got to wear high heels. Phoebe remembers it because she got to see all the soldiers and also was enthralled watching a magician named Sanders whom Mamie Craig had hired for entertainment. Held on a beautiful afternoon, the reception was a big success.

In the early 1940s, W.R. Wills' doctor, Al Harris, died. His successors at City View were less optimistic over Wills' chances of recovery than Harris had been. Before Harris died, Jesse Wills spoke to him about the possibility of moving Wills to another facility. Harris advised against it, saying that "he was well taken care of where he was and it would be very difficult to move him."[73] Jesse also had Dr. William F. Orr from Vanderbilt Hospital come out and examine his father. Orr did so and expressed the opinion that Wills was not manic-depressive but didn't tell Jesse what condition he had.

Jessie Wills went to City View Sanitarium weekly to see her husband. Her chauffeur, Lem Wilson, drove, and occasionally a Clark grandchild accompanied them. When Eleanor, the oldest grandchild, was 10 or 11, Mamma Wills suggested that she go with her and Lem to City View to take Papa Wills some cookies. Eleanor remembered getting out of the car and walking to the front entrance where she rang the doorbell. When someone answered it, she gave him the cookies and asked that he give them to her grandfather. Later, Phoebe and George each accompanied their grandmother on trips to City View to take Wills cookies or some toiletry item. Phoebe and George remembered staying in the car while Lem delivered whatever items were needed.

The Clark and Wills grandchildren were told almost nothing about their grandfather Wills' condition after his breakdown, and the subject was never discussed when the two families had Sunday dinner with Mamma Wills at Far Hills. This may be explained by the fact that in the 1940s, there was a strong social stigma associated with mental illness. Ridley Wills II remembers being told that Papa Wills could never be convinced that America declared war on Germany in December 1941. Eleanor Kelley is certain that her mother visited her grandfather at City View, but it seems clear that Mamie Craig and Jesse visited much less frequently that their mother did. Jesse never talked to his children about his visits, so they have no idea of how often he went. It seems likely that, at some point, Papa Wills no longer recognized his family. That may explain why Phoebe Nischan and George Crook remember Lem delivering cookies and toiletry items while Mrs. Wills stayed in the car.

At a quarterly meeting of the Board of Directors of National Life and Accident Insurance Company in August 1943, Chairman C.A. Craig announced his resignation as board chairman. In the absence of vice

---

73   Letter, Jesse Wills to G. Tivis Graves, Jr., M.D., November 30, 1949.

chairman W.R. Wills, who was still ill, Cecil Sims, a director, assumed the chair. Craig's resignation was accepted and President C. Runcie Clements was elected to succeed Craig as chairman of the board. Edwin W. Craig, Mr. Craig's son, was elected president. The transition to the second generation of executive officers at National Life was under way.

After nearly eight years at City View Sanitarium, the chances of Wills, then 73 years old, recovering were remote. Accordingly, on July 26, 1944, Jesse Wills, Mamie Craig Wills Clark and Jessie Ely Wills instituted guardianship proceedings to enable Jesse to officially act for his father. The first step was to have Wills declared legally incompetent. On August 4, 1944, Thomas A. Shriver, chancellor of the court, "ordered, judged and decreed that Jesse E. Wills is hereby appointed guardian for William Ridley Wills to manage his person and estate, or such part thereof as the Court may from time to time order, with such powers and authority as are contained in this decree." [74]

One of the first steps Jesse took, after becoming guardian, was to sell his father's farm in Williamson County. The farm had earlier proved to be a burden for Jesse because tenants were hard to come by during the war. Several years earlier, however, Jesse had employed Mr. W. D. Jones, to live on the farm and sharecrop. He found Mr. Jones to be honest and dependable. Through one of Jesse's best friends, Vernon Sharp Jr., he sold the farm, with the concurrence of the Chancery Court, to Lt. Campbell H. Brown, then in the U.S. Army stationed at Camp Roberts, California. Douglas Henry, associate general counsel at National Life, drafted the sales document, which was filed January 13, 1945. The sale price was $14,500.

The author's memories of Far Hills during the 1940s when his grandmother lived there alone focused on Sundays when she held court over Sunday dinner for her two children, their spouses and her six grandchildren. Ridley remembered "Xenie, the cook, who made vanilla ice cream and fudge cake; Little Mary, the maid, who helped serve dinner, and Lem, the patient and long-suffering chauffeur, who always announced dinner by walking into the living room with a gong that he banged. This always reminded me of a character out of Terry

---

74   Davidson County Minute Book, 155, page 96.

and the Pirates." Jean Ewing Love remembered seeing Mrs. Wills, during the 1940s, sitting in the back seat of her Packard on Sixth Avenue North in front of B.F. Stief Jewelry Company. Ryan Richardson, who worked there for many years, would bring out several silver pieces for her consideration as wedding presents.

After dinner, Ridley often squabbled with his brother, Matt, or played hide and seek with him, their sister, Ellen, and Phoebe. Cousin George was too little to be very involved, and Eleanor was too old. Even as a small child, George was extremely interested in automobiles and would lie on the floor intently looking at automobile magazines. If the weather was cold, Ellen Wills and Aunt Mamie Craig made their children put on earmuffs and heavy coats before going outside. In the spring and summer, the kids climbed trees, played Tarzan, rode tricycles on the turn-a-round and later bicycles on Curtiswood Lane, sometimes with Peggy Smith, a friend of Ellen's, who lived down the street. They waded in the creek that meandered through the Smiths' front yard.[75] Occasionally, the children would jump in the reflector pool despite being warned not to do so. They stayed clear of Mamma Wills' prized rose garden, where she grew bush and climbing roses, both of which had nasty thorns. Ellen Martin remembered sitting under the wisteria vines that were in the yard and how beautiful they were. In inclement weather, the children played in the attic, rode roller skates on the black-and-white marble floor in the entrance hall or played with World War II toy soldiers from the toy chest.

On the occasional weekends when Ridley would spend Saturday night with Mamma Wills, he would sleep in the bedroom over the kitchen, a long way down the hall from his grandmother's room. Sometimes, she and Ridley would listen to The Shadow Knows or The Lone Ranger on the Mutual Radio Network. After "Wiggie" got in bed, Mother Wills would tuck him in, turn off the light and walk down the long hall to the other end of the house. It was a little scary for Ridley, but his grandmother never seemed the least bit afraid of living alone.

Mamie Craig and Ted Clark's marriage began to unravel during the

---

75 Margaret "Peggy" Smith was the daughter of Margaret Thompson and E. Laird Smith, and the granddaughter of Mother Wills' friend, Margaret Lipscomb (Mrs. Overton) Thompson.

war. Much more outgoing than his wife, Ted enjoyed having drinks with friends. Sometimes, he came home late with alcohol on his breath and there would be shouting matches as there were questions in Mamie Craig's mind as to where and with whom he had been. Mamma Wills would usually invite her children and grandchildren to have Sunday dinner at Far Hills. Ted hated attending these formal affairs and would often arrive late, strolling casually across the yard between the two houses, dressed fashionably in a smoking jacket instead of the Sunday suit that Jesse always wore. This naturally irked

Mamie Craig Clark and her mother, Mrs. Jessie Ely Wills, 1940s

Mamma Wills. Feeling that life with Ted was too unsettling, Mamie Craig divorced him on June 29, 1944, even though she still loved him. Under the divorce settlement, she got full custody of their three children but no financial support. That meant her only income was about $5,000 annually from the trust her father set up in 1929. Pretty soon thereafter, Mamie Craig, and her three children moved to a rented house on Evelyn Avenue in Belle Meade.

With Wills still in City View Sanitarium and with little possibility of him ever recovering, Mrs. Jessie Wills relied on E. Gray Smith, who ran the Packard dealership on West End Avenue, for all matters regarding cars. When her Packard broke down or needed service, she called Smith, who would send Sam Henderson out to Far Hills to pick up her car and leave one for her chauffeur, Lem Wilson, to drive while her Packard was being serviced. When she was ready to trade her car for a new model, Smith would bring a new car out to Far Hills to see if it met her approval. Mamma Wills' grandson, George W. Crook, remembers when he was five or six, that Smith brought four or five new Packards out for Mrs. Wills to choose between. When granddaughter Eleanor Clark got her driver's license, she drove her mother's white Packard around and around the circle at Far Hills' front entrance. Enjoying the ride were Phoebe and George, who were not about to be left out, and probably two or three Wills first cousins. Of course, the ride was short-lived as Mamie Craig soon was at the front door telling Eleanor, in no uncertain terms, to stop.

On August 14, 1944, only 10 days after he had been named guardian for his father, Jesse Wills petitioned the Chancery Court of Davidson County, on behalf of himself and his sister, Mamie Craig Clark, to allocate from their father's estate, that had a $3,518,655 market value, 25,000 shares of Associated National Trustees stock to the each of them. The value of the stock was then $22.00 per share. So, the gifts would each be worth $550,000. The stock paid a dividend of 65 cents a share, patterned after the dividend rate of National Life stock. After hearing the testimony of Jesse Wills, J. Mac Peebles, C.A. Craig, Runcie Clements, and Miss Margaret Crecelius, Wills' secretary, and satisfying himself that Ridley Wills reduced assets would be sufficient to meet the needs of his wife, Jessie Ely Wills, and pay his expenses at City View Sanitarium,[76] the Honorable Thomas A. Shriver, Chancellor, granted the petition.

In 1946, Mamie Craig met Senter C. Crook, who was living in Colorado but had come to Nashville for a visit. Senter's first cousin, Celeste Hale (Mrs. Walker) Casey introduced them. Senter also had a half-sister, Martha Crook, who was in her senior year at Vanderbilt and another first cousin, Celeste's brother, Walter Hale, living there. Senter, who was the one in his generation to keep up with family, also had many Nashville friends whom he had known since his undergraduate days at Vanderbilt.

Born in 1898, Senter was educated in the public schools of Jackson before entering Vanderbilt in the fall of 1916. A good athlete, he played forward on the varsity basketball team his freshman and sophomore years and doubled up as team manager the second year. Senter also won the school tennis doubles championship and was a member of Phi Delta Theta, Nemo Club and the Philosophic Literary Society. He had plans to follow in the footsteps of his father, Dr. Jere Crook, by going to Vanderbilt Medical School. Those plans were struck down when he

---

76 Jesse Wills testified in Chancery Court in August 1944 that the total cost of keeping his father in City View Sanitarium was a little over $400 a month. This included his board and bed, upkeep, nursing care, doctors' bills and clothing.

developed tuberculosis during his junior year. He left school and moved to Colorado, where a lung was removed and where he lived, in 1923, at 12 Long Apartments in Fort Collins, and later, in Boulder. Always loyal to Vanderbilt, he attended the first Vanderbilt Alumni meeting ever held in Colorado at the Shirley-Savoy Hotel in Denver in the mid-1920s. In late 1945 or early 1946, Senter's doctor in Denver said that his tuberculosis was no longer active. This opened the way for Senter to move back to Jackson.

On of the first things Senter did, after becoming engaged to Mamie Craig in 1946, was to go to the Theta House at Vanderbilt and tell his half-sister, Martha, the exciting news. He insisted that Mamie Craig go with him to see his physician in Denver to satisfy herself that he was tuberculosis-free. "While out there, why not get married at the Broadmoor Hotel in Colorado Springs?" he asked. Mamie Craig agreed, and they were married June 21, 1946, at the Broadmoor. Mamie Craig's daughter, Eleanor, recalls that "Maymay" (Mamie Craig's nickname) "went out of town and came back with Senter." She said to her children, "Here's my new husband."

Senter C. Cook (1898–1965)

Senter Crook proved to be a fine husband and a wonderful stepfather to Mamie Craig's children, particularly to Phoebe and George, the two youngest. Senter actually adopted George who changed his last name from Clark to Crook. A few months after their marriage, Senter and Mamie Craig moved with her children to his hometown of Jackson. There, in the fall of 1946, Eleanor entered the sophomore class at Jackson High School, Phoebe entered the eighth grade at Jackson Junior high and George entered grammar school. The Crooks rented an attractive two-story, brick home on a hill sloping down to the Humboldt Highway, later renamed Highland Avenue.

While living in Jackson, Mamie Craig and the children frequently came back to Nashville for social events and for medical appointments.

142

Because she was a teenager, Eleanor would sometimes come by herself and stay at Far Hills with Mamma Wills, who was closer to her than she was to her other, younger grandchildren.

At Thanksgiving 1946, Jesse and Ellen brought their three children to Jackson for a visit. Mother Wills also went along, anxious to see her grandchildren. Ellen Wills Martin remembered in 2008 that she and other family members went walking in the woods behind the Crooks' home after Thanksgiving dinner. The following spring, Senter's half brother, Angus Crook, only three years older than Eleanor Clark, returned from the service and found Senter living in Jackson with his new family. Angus, who reentered the University of the South that spring, invited the 16-year-old Eleanor there for a weekend.

With three grandchildren, whom she had been very close to, living out of town, Mamma Wills sometimes invited her Wills grandchildren to spend the night with her. "Little Ellen," whom the family called "Baby Sis," came on Saturday night, February 16, 1947. Although Ellen, then 10 years old, had pretty much outgrown her fear of sleeping in a bedroom so far down the hall from her grandmother's room, she was shocked when she went in Mamma Wills' bedroom on Sunday morning and found her crying. The headline on the Sunday morning *Tennessean*, lying on the bed, told the story. Five close friends of Mrs. Wills had been killed Saturday night when their automobile had been struck by a Nashville-bound passenger train at the Nashville, Chattanooga & St. Louis crossing on Old Harding Road. The victims, all prominent Nashvillians, were headed for dinner at the Belle Meade Country Club. They were Mr. and Mrs. Johnson Bransford, Mrs. Richard W. "Julia" Dake, Mr. Pat Mann Estes, and Mrs. Edwin Warner. Pat Estes was also a cousin of Ridley Wills.

For many years, Senter and Mamie Craig rented houses in Douglas, Michigan, a fashionable summer resort on Lake Michigan. Senter had a boat there and even got a small boat with a motor for George to ride around on one of the small lakes in the area. George and Phoebe went to St. John's and Camp Nagawicka, sister camps in Delafield, Wisconsin, some of the years that their mother and stepfather were at Douglas. In July, 1949, the Wills visited the Crooks at Douglas. That same summer, Mamie Craig offered Senter's first cousin, Martha Crook Thompson, her husband, Joe, and their 1-month-old daughter, Mindy, the Crooks' house on Sheppard Place for two weeks while they were at Douglas. The Thompsons, who were then living in a small duplex on Brighton Avenue without air conditioning, were grateful and accepted. The Crooks did have air conditioning.

Ridley Wills' closest relative in Brownsville, Eva Mann Moore, died in March 1945. The widow of William D. Moore, she was buried in Oakwood Cemetery next to her husband and her parents – Martha Epps and Asa Mann. A month later, on April 10, Ellen's father, Dr. Matt Buckner died of cancer at age 74. He had practiced medicine in Nashville for 48 years and had worked with Wills on the Session at First Presbyterian. Matt's widow, Elizabeth, died 22 months later at age 70.

In 1946, Mamie Craig asked her mother and brother to petition the Chancery Court for permission to sell the home on Curtiswood next door to Far Hills where Mamie Craig and her family had lived from 1941 until 1944. Jesse and Mrs. Wills did so, selling the house and its five-acre lot to Kermit C. Stengel for $57,000. The court approved the sale, on March 22, 1946, and also the purchase by Ridley and Jessie Wills of a house on Honeywood Avenue that Mamie Craig moved to when she and Senter returned to Nashville from Jackson. For it, they paid $32,500 in cash. In 1947, Mrs. Wills and Jesse sold the house on Honeywood, and Mrs. Wills bought for Mamie Craig an attractive two-story house on the southwest corner of Sheppard Place and Jackson Boulevard that cost $32,250.

When the Crooks moved back to Nashville in 1948, Eleanor had just finished her junior year in high school. That fall, she transferred to Holton Arms Girls' School in Washington, D.C., where her mother had gone. Eleanor completed high school there and went on to graduate from Holton Arms Junior College two years later. Phoebe and George returned to Nashville with their mother and stepfather. There, Phoebe attended Ward Belmont for two years before transferring to Holton Arms, where she graduated from high school in 1951 and junior college in 1953. At Senter's urging, Phoebe attended Vanderbilt for one year after graduating from Holton Arms. George went to Parmer School. He later graduated from Oxford Academy in Pleasantville, N.J. and from Rollins College.

144

CHAPTER XII

A MOVE TO BELLE MEADE & RIDLEY'S DEATH

Nashville Realtor Earl Woolwine approached Jesse Wills and his mother, Jessie Wills, in 1947 about their interest in selling Far Hills to the State of Tennessee for an executive residence. They agreed for him to negotiate with the State Commission as their agent, provided Mrs. Wills was given sufficient time to find another home, and agreed on a sale price of $125,000. Wills recalled, in 1948, that the State Commission never visited the house, although Mr. Woolwine did. At the same time, Woolwine and other Realtors were discussing with the state other possible homes as prospective executive residences. Wills understood that Gov. and Mrs. Jim McCord were not interested in Far Hills or any of the other houses. The committee took no action, and Wills considered the matter closed.

In the summer of 1948, Jesse Wills persuaded his mother, who dearly loved Far Hills, to move a smaller house in Belle Meade where she would be much closer to him and Mamie Craig and, more importantly, to her grandchildren. Having had a good experience with prominent Nashville Realtor Barrington Criddle in 1947, when he helped Mrs. Wills and Jesse buy the house for Mamie Craig on Sheppard Place, she and Jesse gave Criddle exclusive rights to sell Far Hills. Through him, Mrs. Wills bought, in September, a house at 709 Belle Meade Blvd. Criddle put half-page ads in both *The Nashville Tennessean* and the *Nashville Banner*. The top half of the ad featured a picture of Far Hills from the front lawn. The caption was designed to catch your eye. "One of the Most Outstanding Palatial Estates in Nashville or Even in Tennessee...Only $125,000.00...Inspection by appointment only. Situated on Curtis Wood Lane about one-fourth miles from Franklin Road in a very select area and surrounded by other handsome estates." The ad then described the rooms on the three floors of the house described as Georgian Colonial. Nashville attorney Jack Norman Sr. noticed the ad while reading *The Nashville Tennessean* at his breakfast table. He knew that the state legislature had already decreed the executive residence at 2118 West End Ave. no longer suitable for the chief executive of the state. He thought to himself, "Why not buy Far Hills?" He called governor-to-be

Gordon Browning and found him to be just as reluctant as McCord had been. Browning told Norman that, "If I spent that kind of money on a mansion, the people of Tennessee would run me out of the state." A kitchen accident at the residence on West End may have made Mrs. Browning more receptive to the idea of a new house than her husband. One day she was cooking on a wood-burning stove in the kitchen when the flue broke. Soot covered everything. Mrs. Browning was so exasperated that she said, "Gordon, you've got to find us a decent place to live." He did.

The left lead article on the front page of *The Nashville Tennessean*, on November 25, 1948, carried the headline: "State Will Buy Wills Property for Mansion Use." The article said negotiations would be completed in a few days and that Gov. and Mrs. Browning had inspected the property and approved its purchase. Two purchase possibilities were being discussed by state officials – an outright purchase and a trade-in of the present executive mansion at 2118 West End Ave. to the Wills. It was understood that Browning would move into the residence when "he becomes governor in January." Earlier, the state abandoned the idea of using Brentwood Hall, former estate of Rogers Caldwell, as a governor's mansion. The state had recently bought it for $150,000, the article stated.

The Nashville Tennessean article was correct. The next day, a State board created by Chapter 159 of the Public Acts of 1947 submitted a written proposal to buy Far Hills and 10.436 acres, as well as listed personal property, from the estate of Ridley Wills for $120,350 – $90,350 upon delivery of the deed and $30,000 on or before April 1, 1949. There was no mention of a land swap involving the old executive residence; the Wills were not interested. Jim McCord, governor, and Gordon Browning, governor-elect, both signed the document, as did Joe C. Carr, secretary of state; Sam Carson, commissioner of finance and taxation; Jared Maddux, comptroller; J. F. Murrey, treasurer; and Roy H. Beeler, attorney general.

When the public announcement was made that the W.R. Wills home had been purchased by the State of Tennessee as a new executive residence, Nashvillians came in droves to see the house. Some of the cars lined up, bumper to bumper, on narrow Curtiswood Lane and turned around in the driveway of Mr. and Mrs. Andrew Benedict Jr., almost directly across the street. Andrew "Buddy" Benedict III, then about 6, thought the sightseers had mistaken his house for the executive residence. He pulled a little stool down to the end of his driveway and patiently explained to the sightseers that the governor lived across the street.

Earl G. Woolwine, president of Green Hills-Belle Meade Realtors, was one of those who read the story of the sale in the newspaper. His immediate reaction was that he deserved the commission on the $120,350 purchase price. He wrote Jesse Wills to make the following argument:

> The property was duly and regularly listed with me for sale; I originated as prospective purchaser the State of Tennessee and first made a contact with the purchasing committee; The deal has now been closed and property transferred to the State of Tennessee.

Therefore, I am of the opinion that I am legally and morally entitled to the agent's commission on the sale.

Two days later, Jesse Wills wrote Woolwine, acknowledging the receipt of his letter of December 4, 1948. Jesse's response was that, in view of the fact that both he and Criddle were claiming the commission for the sale, "if and when the sale is complete, I, as guardian of my father's estate, and my mother, acting upon the advise of our counsel, expect to file a bill of interpleader in the Chancery court of Davidson County, Tennessee and pay the amount of this commission into the registry of the Chancery Court, so that the Court may decide to whom the commission is due."

On January 15, 1949, Jesse Wills and C.B. Criddle paid Hillsboro-Belle Meade Realty Company, Earl G. Woolwine, president, $500 and $250, respectively. In exchange for the $750 payment, Mr. Woolwine signed a full release of all claims against Mrs. Jessie Wills, Jesse Wills, or C.B. Criddle. Jesse felt that he had dodged a bullet.

A few days later, Douglas Henry wrote Jesse to say, "Everything in connection with the sale of Far Hills to the State has been completed. The deed was delivered to the Sate. The State delivered to me two checks, one for $100,000 and one for $21,331.08. These checks were endorsed and deposited in the Jesse Wills Guardian account. You delivered me three checks – one for $6,550 payable to C.B. Criddle; and two payable to Douglas Henry; one for $350 and another for $500. The $350 check was endorsed by me to the Guaranty Title Company. The check for $500 was endorsed by me to Earl G. Woolwine and George H. Cate and was delivered to Woolwine with C.B. Criddle's check for $250. For this $750 we obtained from Woolwine and Hillsboro-Belle Meade Realty Co. a full release of all claims against Mr. Wills, Mrs. Wills, you or C.B. Riddle because of the sale."

Sometime after Gov. and Mrs. Gordon Browning moved to Far Hills, Mrs. Browning called Mrs. Wills, then 76, and invited her to come and see the house and the rose garden that had been Mrs. Wills' pride and joy. Mamma Wills traveled out there, driven by Lem Wilson. Later, she told her granddaughter, Eleanor, what a lovely lady Mrs. Browning was and that she was glad she was living at Far Hills and looking after her roses. Mamma Wills was not as happy when another governor's wife white washed the lead statuary in the front lawn.

In the midst of his negotiations with the State of Tennessee, Jesse received a letter from Della Wills, Mann's widow. He knew how alone she felt during the 12 years after Mann's death and Ridley's breakdown. Jesse had kept up with her primarily through Della's daughter, Trousdale Wills Sturdivant, who lived with her husband, Robert, at 3812 Richland Ave. in Nashville. The fact that Della was living with Elizabeth in Memphis gave everyone in the family comfort. In her letter to Jesse, written November 11, 1948, Della asked for financial assistance. She said she had been left only a few thousand dollars when Mann died. She then explained that things improved a bit in 1940 when she received $6,500 in life insurance benefits and $4,200 for selling her house, although that, she felt, was a low price because there was still very little money

Trousdale Wills (Mrs. Robert) Sturdivant (1894–1975

circulating in Brownsville and the house was in poor repair. For a few years before Mann's death, she said, "He was sick and unable to attend to his business." Jesse knew some of this background information, but not being nearly as tuned into Brownsville as his father had been, he was caught off guard, when Della said, "Your father had been sending him $150 per month for some time before his death."

Four days later, Jesse wrote his aunt Della saying he had delayed writing until he had a chance to talk to Trousdale, "which I did yesterday afternoon." He said he had not shown Della's letter to his mother because "she is somewhat harassed and worried at present over the sale of the big house and moving to a smaller one in Belle Meade." He said work was being done on the Belle Meade house and that she hoped to be in by Christmas. He then explained the status of his father's affairs. He said that he and the Chancery Court had been appointed as co-guardians of his father and that, as a consequence, he was "sharply limited with what I can do with his funds." Annually he had to make a report to the court accounting for all income and expenditures and had to turn over annually to the court every check he had written on his father's account. For example, he told Della he could no longer make charitable contributions out of the account and that the court dictated how much allowance he could give his mother. He had to go to court to help out his sister who had little financial means after her divorce. He could not make annual gifts, for his father, to Mr. Wills' grandchildren that would have helped reduce his estate and the terrific inheritance tax the estate would have to pay when Mr. Wills died. He said that he had also been involved in a disagreement with the government over gift taxes, part of which related to the trust W.R. Wills set up in 1929 to benefit Jesse and Mamie Craig. The point of all this, he said, was to say "no matter how much I might want to I can't legally help anybody out of dad's estate." Jesse told Della that he had considerable means of his own and that he was interested in the family. He said he had given his nephew, Ridley, money three times in the past 18 months with his own money. He said that he had talked to Trousdale to determine if "there was any emergency anywhere in the family." Trousdale said she did not think there was. Jesse suggested that Della speak to Trousdale "so she can talk things over with me." Jesse also mentioned that he had helped Virginia stay in Vanderbilt, where she was president of Kappa Alpha Theta Sorority.

Della wrote Jesse on December 6, thanking him for his nice letter and saying that she did not understand the situation. She said she would keep Trousdale informed of her needs and that "Harriette and Elizabeth may be in a position to help me too." She thanked Jesse "for your patience and kindness. We certainly," she continued, "appreciate your helping Ridley. I don't know what would become of him, except for you. I hold you in the highest esteem."

Ridley Wills had been at City View Sanitarium 12 years when his wife and son sold Far Hills. He never knew that they had done so. In the summer of 1949, G. Tivis Graves Jr., M.D., neuropsychiatrist there, wrote Jesse Wills furnishing him with a medical report on his father. Graves wrote "there does not seem to be any appreciable change in Mr. Wills' condition at this time. It appears to Dr. [Will] Camp and me he has had numerous small brain hemorrhages and/or small areas of brain softening." He estimated that Wills had "something like 15 or 16 since the beginning of this last illness." He said they were making every effort to keep him comfortable and that "he is suffering very little." For the past four weeks, Graves said they had been giving Wills occasional sedatives and frequent narcotics to keep him comfortable. "He still gets considerable relief from as little as one-ninth of a grain of morphine, which is most encouraging." Graves wrote that Wills had not resisted treatment "to any considerable degree during the past few weeks." He could not, however, predict the duration of the illness. Graves added that they "were giving him hypodermic injections of vitamins because he was taking insufficient vitamins by mouth." He ended by saying, "We wish to take this opportunity to thank you again for your thoughtful and wholehearted cooperation." During the fall, Wills' condition worsened.

On November 19, Wills suffered a stroke. The end came quickly and peacefully two days later. Dr. Tivis Graves Jr. called Jesse Wills about 6:30 a.m. on November 21, 1949, to inform him that his father had passed away at 6:18 that morning. In a letter written later that day, Graves said "Mr. Wills passing was without any struggle and without any spoken word. He just passed quietly as though in continued sleep." He said that, during the past several months when Wills was so critically ill, "we have been able to keep him comfortable the greater part of the

150

time by supplying him the necessary sedatives and analgesics, excellent nursing care, special injections of fluid and food, but most of all because all of us had a sincere desire to aid in his personal comfort in every way." He then wrote, "We wish to take this opportunity to thank all of you for your intelligent, considerate understanding and whole-hearted cooperation through all this long and difficult period of illness. It has made a very difficult task easier for us. Dr. Camp and all of the nurses express their personal appreciation to you."

Ridley Wills' funeral service was at his wife's home on Belle Meade Boulevard on November 22. Dr. Walter R. Courtenay officiated. Pallbearers were Edwin W. Craig, E.B. Stevenson Jr., Douglas Henry, Rufus E. Fort Jr., G. Henry Tyne, J.M. Peebles, Dr. B.F. Byrd, Walter S. Bearden Jr., E.L Stritch, G.C. Lynch and Horace T. Polk, all senior officers at National Life.[77] Honorary pallbearers were elders at First Presbyterian Church. Flowers filled the dining and living rooms. In addition to having her family with her, Mrs. Wills had the support of her dear friend, Mrs. Elizabeth Dibrell, whom everyone called "Mother Dear."

When *The Brownsville States-Graphic* came out on Friday, its front page featured a notice of Ridley Wills' death and comments on how much this man had meant to Haywood County.

Jesse Wills wrote Graves, thanking him and the other staff members at City View for the care they had given Wills for approximately 13 years. Jesse expressed uncertainty about the nature of his father's psychosis, realizing how much was unknown about mental illness. He asked Graves if there were many cases that last so long as did Wills' depressive state. He also asked if his father ever talked to them about what might have brought on the depression. On December 2, Graves responded to Jesse Wills' letter. He said he thought the manic-depressive psychosis diagnosis made in the 1920s by Drs. Stephens and Harris was correct. He said statistics were that the average depressive stage lasted 2.2 years but that he had seen cases to last five years. He felt the 1936 breakdown was also manic-depressive psychosis and at that time "the

---

77 Walter S. Bearden's mother, Margaret "Maggie" Whiteside Bearden, and Susan Whiteside Cooper were sisters of Ruth Whiteside Ely.

illness was complicated by the onset of an involuntary melancholia state in addition to a progressive cerebral arteriosclerosis." Graves felt these complications were responsible for his lack of recovery and his death. As to the cause of the nervous breakdown, Graves wrote, "This type of illness is produced from the overall picture of the patient's attempt to push himself at work, his physical health, and the nervous system that he was born with." Graves said he had been studying Wills' case for approximately three years.

Because of his illness, Ridley Wills was unable to make estate plans during the last 13 years of his life, and he died without a will. Consequently, his estate paid a heavy penalty in death taxes. This prompted Jesse Wills to start making annual gifts to his three children. He also sold a great deal of National Life stock to settle his father's estate. Sam Fleming, vice president of Third National Bank, wrote Frank Farris, the bank's CEO, then convalescing at Fort Meyers, Florida, suggesting that the bank buy some of that stock. Farris responded by saying, "Your reasoning regarding the Wills stock sounds reasonable to me." Eldon Stevenson, Jr., a younger colleague at National Life, also bought some of Wills' stock.

CHAPTER XIII

THE FINAL YEARS

Ridley Wills' great nephew, Mann Wills Oglesby, named for his grandfather, and Mary Jane Millard married in her hometown of Memphis on November 5, 1949. Wills and Mary Jane would make wonderful places for themselves in Nashville, where he would become assistant treasurer at Genesco. They have three children, John Wills Oglesby, an orthopedic surgeon in Nashville; Robert Edwin Oglesby, a Nashville architect; and Jane Millard Oglesby Jones, a pediatrician who practices medicine in Chattanooga and lives on Signal Mountain with her husband, Andrew Roy Jones, M.D., who also practices medicine in Chattanooga as an OB/GYN.

The three children would never know their Oglesby grandmother. She was killed in a two-car automobile crash in 1955 while driving with her husband, Herbert, to their home in Memphis late at night from their fishing cabin on Horseshoe Lake in Arkansas. The cause of the accident was never determined. Herbert, 58, a real estate developer in Memphis, was severely injured, and he lived the remaining 16 years of his life as a paraplegic.[78] Wills had been with his parents at the lake only two weeks earlier. On the way back to Memphis, while crossing the Harahan Bridge over the Mississippi River, Harriette began telling him what disposition she wanted to make of certain possessions at her death. Wills asked her why she wanted to talk about that when she was only 54 years old.

Mindful of her own mortality, Mrs. Jessie Ely Wills made and published her last will and testament on July 2, 1950. She left to her son, Jesse, and daughter, Mamie Craig Wills Crook, equally, all her household furniture, rugs, personal effects, jewelry, portraits, automobiles and such. Jesse Wills was executor of the will, which was witnessed by Mrs. Wills'

---

78   Later, when Mae Cox Wisdom, whom Herbert Exum Oglesby knew when they both worked for the bank in Jackson, Tenn., found out that he was a paraplegic living in a nursing home with an attendant, she came to see him and asked him to marry her. A wealthy widow, with no children, Mrs. Oglesby said she did so out of Christian charity toward someone she admired and respected. Because of her generosity, Herbert's life was much happier than it otherwise would have been. Among other kindnesses toward Herbert, Mae Oglesby took him and his attendant on cruises to Hawaii and the Mediterranean.

attorney and her husband's great nephew, Robert Wills Sturdivant, and J.M. Peebles.

In December of that year, Mrs. Wills took a bolder estate-planning step. She (the settler) transferred 18,000 shares of National Life and Accident Insurance company stock to the First American National Bank, trustee, establishing two trusts, one that would pay the net income to her son, Jesse, during his lifetime and, on his death, to his lineal descendants, per stirpes. "On the death of the last of the following named persons: settler's son, Jesse E. Wills, settler's grandchildren: Matthew Buckner Wills, William Ridley Wills II, and Ellen McClung Wills, this trust shall terminate and the corpus and any undistributed income shall be distributed among the lineal descendants of settler's said son, Jesse E. Wills, per stirpes." The other trust, benefiting her daughter, Mamie Craig Crook, during her lifetime, would, upon Mamie Craig's death, pay the net income to her descendants: Eleanor Wills Clark, Phoebe Clark and George Wills Crook. The termination clause worked the same way as the Wills trust. Robert Wills Sturdivant drafted these trusts.

Mamie Craig's first husband, Clinton Pennington "Ted" Clark, died December 29, 1951, in Fort Lauderdale, Florida, of a massive hemorrhage due to cirrhosis of the liver, a condition he had fought for 10 years. Sadly, he never got to see his daughter Teddy, who was born the same day he died. At the time of his death, he was only 52. Until then, he and his second wife, Jennie Davis Clark, were living in Fort Lauderdale. He had outlived his mother, Phebe Eastgate Clark, by only nine years.[79] Eleanor, Phoebe and George seldom saw their father after the divorce. George remembered seeing him twice. Once, soon after the divorce, Clark drove out to Mamie Craig's house in a yellow Pontiac pulling a yellow trailer. He picked up his son and took him to get an ice cream cone. Later, on at least two occasions, Clark had made efforts to see his children from his first marriage. On one such occasion, four years before his death, Ted wrote William P. Cooper, his lawyer in Nashville, asking if he could see Eleanor, Phoebe and George. Senter Crook responded by letter on April 5, 1947. He wrote he did not want

---

79   Mrs. Phebe Eastgate Clark was living at 2316 Dixie Place in Nashville at the time of her death on January 8, 1942. She was 70 years old.

Clark to see his children because it would upset their mother. In the years after Ted's death, Mamie Craig would periodically drive out to Mt. Olivet Cemetery with her best friend Frances Bell to see his grave.

Jesse wrote Mamie Craig in August 1952 to explain the difficulty the Bank of New York had in dividing up the bonds and other securities that were in their father's trust – one half of which went to Mrs. Wills and 1/4 each to Jesse and Mamie Craig. He said that he and Robert Wills Sturdivant, by then Jesse's lawyer, had worked hard to make the division equitable both as to principal and income. Jesse enclosed a form for her to sign if she agreed with the division. By July 1, 1952, the Bank of New York had created three trusts, one for Mrs. Wills, one for Mamie Craig and one for Jesse.

T. Leigh Thompson wrote Jesse and Ellen from Wild Rose Farm, near Lewisburg, to thank them for *A Natural History of Trees* they sent him for Christmas 1951. The last paragraph in Uncle Leigh's hand was as follows: "I cherish with many happy memories the years of your childhood and young manhood. I would like to see you president of the National Life and Accident Insurance Company." A year later, Jesse was named Executive Vice president of National Life. In 1953, before Jesse became president of National Life, Thompson died at his winter home in St. Petersburg, Florida. He was 91. His remains were returned to Lewisburg, where his funeral was held and where he was buried in Lone Oak Cemetery. Thompson was survived by his second wife, Dee Turrentine Thompson. Jesse and Ellen, who once took their children to see Thompson and the trees he planted at Wild Rose Farm when he was an octogenarian, attended his funeral. Maybe Jesse thought about the time, decades earlier, when he went by train to visit his uncle at Wild Rose Farm. Jesse always remembered that, on that memorial trip, he changed trains in Columbia and then traveled to Lewisburg on an old wood-burning train with a funnel smokestack.

Vanderbilt Memorial Gymnasium was dedicated on Saturday evening, December 6, 1952. Madison Sarratt, vice chancellor of the university and chairman of the advisory committee on Athletics and Physical Education, presided. Charles Ragland, general chairman of the Memorial Gymnasium Campaign, presented the gymnasium to Vanderbilt. Chancellor Harvey Branscomb accepted the gymnasium, and trustee James G. Stahlman gave the memorial address. John Keith Benton, dean of the School of Religion, gave the prayer of dedication. Jesse and Ellen Wills were there for the dedication and for the game with the University of Virginia that followed.

The Wills had season tickets for basketball for many years. Jesse's mother, Jessie Wills, also had basketball season tickets in the 1950s. She regularly attended games with her close friend, Mrs. Elizabeth "Mother Dear" Dibrell. After the games, Mr. and Mrs. Wills would sometimes follow the two elderly ladies to make sure they reached Mrs. Dibrell's car safely. Jessie and Elizabeth were often seen on Belle Meade Boulevard, with Mrs. Dibrell behind the wheel, as she would not hire a chauffeur until she was nearly 90. People who knew both ladies would sometimes pull up behind Mrs. Dibrell's car and stare intently to be certain that someone was behind the wheel. Mrs. Dibrell and Mrs. Wills were so diminutive; they could hardly be seen from the rear.

Although dear friends, Jessie and Elizabeth spoke very directly to each other, never reluctant to say exactly what they thought. The Belle Meade Police were quite aware that Mrs. Dibrell exceeded the speed limit with regularity despite being an octogenarian. One policeman said, "I never would give her a ticket, but every once in a while I would stop her and ask her to slow down."

Della Womack Wills, the widow of Asa Mann Wills, passed away in 1953. She was laid to rest in Brownsville's Oakwood Cemetery. Her son, Ridley, died at Bay Pines not long after. Ridley's ex-wife, Luella, died in Honolulu on April 13, 1959. Robert "Pappy" Sturdivant, died September 21, 1954, at age 62. He had moved to Nashville on December 18, 1929, to become a farm inspector in National Life's Mortgage Loan Department. When National Life withdrew from the farm loan business in 1946, Pappy, who always smoked a pipe, was named supervisor of the home office parking lot. There he ran a tight ship and did not take sass from anyone, including country music stars headed for WSM's studios on the fifth floor or, worse, to the Elk's Club on Sixth Avenue North, where there was liquor. Occasionally, one of them would incur Sturdivant's wrath by parking in a space behind the five-story building reserved for one of the company's executive officers. Once, Sturdivant got in a fight with a much younger musician, much to the amusement of his many friends in the home office.

Sturdivant was survived by his widow, Trousdale, and their four children – Robert Wills Sturdivant, a prominent Nashville attorney; Elizabeth (Mrs. Watson) Sims of New York City; Trousdale (Mrs. Erwin S.) Jackson of Washington, D.C., and Virginia (Mrs. K. Harlan, Jr.) Dodson of Nashville. He also was survived by a sister, Mrs. Tom Ott, of Hot Springs, Arkansas, and nine grandchildren.

Bettie's husband, Watson Sims, was an executive and foreign correspondent with Associated Press in Europe and Asia. While they lived in India, she worked for the Fulbright Foundation. They later lived in Asheville, North Carolina.[80] Trousdale was married to Erwin Jackson, a captain in the U.S. Navy, who graduated from the U.S. Naval Academy.[81] Virginia, like her brother, Bob, stayed in Nashville. Her husband, Harlan Dodson Jr., was a respected Nashville attorney, a former state senator, president of the Nashville Chamber of Commerce and president of the Nashville and Tennessee Bar Associations. Harlan's most lasting contribution to the city may have been his service as one of 10 members of the Metro Charter Commission that established the Charter for Metropolitan government on April 6, 1962. During the campaign for Metropolitan government, Harlan actively supported the charter and answered questions submitted to the *Tennessean*'s question and answer column.[82]

Dr. Walter R. Courtenay, the pastor of First Presbyterian Church and the minister who had conducted Ridley Wills' funeral service in 1949, never had been sold on the idea of the historic church remaining downtown, where parking was difficult, where coal dust and soot were problems, and where, he felt, First Church was at a disadvantage in attracting young people who could more easily attend Westminster Presbyterian or some other church in Nashville's western suburbs. Having purchased the John H. Cheek Home, Oak Hill and 50 acres on the Franklin Pike on May 1, 1949, for $116,000, the church built a

---

80   Bettie and Watson Sims had two children: Elizabeth "Holly" Hollister and Winfield Sims.

81   Trousdale and Erwin Jackson had three children: Katherine, Susan and Robert Jackson.

82   Virginia and Harlan's children were Harlan Dodson III, Virginia Marie Dodson Maxwell and John Christopher Dodson.

school there called Oak Hill Country Day School. It opened that fall. Beginning on Mother's Day, May 13, 1950, an early church service at 9 a.m. was held at Oak Hill. Soon, arguments arose among the church officers over whether to spend money on badly needed improvements downtown or to enlarge the chapel and build an education building at Oak Hill. Courtenay, who was at Oak Hill and again two hours later downtown each Sunday morning, dreamed of building a sanctuary and Sunday School building at Oak Hill and moving the church there. At a congregational meeting November 7, 1954, 673 members voted in favor of relocation, with 327 against. The Adams, Cheshire and Wills families were among the most prominent in the minority group. Most young families with children wanted to move, while their aging parents generally wanted to remain where they had been much of their lives. With the decision made to relocate, the minority group reconstituted itself as The Downtown Presbyterian Church and, over time, reached an agreement with First Church to buy the Egyptian Revival Church building on the corner of Fifth Avenue North and Church Street, then 104 years old, from First Church for $550,000. Had it not been for Jesse Wills' $100,000 gift, this would have been impossible. At the first meeting of The Downtown Presbyterian Church on June 5, 1955, Jesse and Ellen Wills were in attendance. That same month, Mrs. Ridley Wills, her son, Jesse Wills, his wife, Ellen, and their children, Ridley and Ellen, moved their memberships to The Downtown Presbyterian Church.[83]

On June 7, Thomas Heron Mitchell, an elder at First Presbyterian Church, wrote Jesse Wills to inform him that, the night before, the First Church Session accepted with regret Jesse's resignation as trustee and treasurer of benevolences. Mitchell spoke of comments made by several people of the fine service Jesse had rendered the church and added, "For many years I have looked upon you as being the most influential man in the church."

A day later, Edwin F. Hunt, a ruling elder at First Presbyterian, wrote Jesse to thank him for sending him a copy of Wills' talk to the Couples Class on May 28, 1955. Hunt wrote, "The sentiments expressed are so

---

83   Matt Wills did not move his church membership because, in 1955, he was serving in the U.S. Army and was not in Nashville.

generous and Christian and, I want to add, typical of you. One of the most distressing aspects of the division in our church for me has been that it will place us in separate congregations."

Meanwhile in Brownsville, the increasing patient load at Haywood County Memorial Hospital necessitated the securing of a grant from Hill Burton funds to double the hospital's bed capacity to 50, add new surgical and obstetrical suites, add new lab and X-ray facilities, add other equipment and renovate the existing building.

Elizabeth Wills, Jesse's first cousin, who was a trustee of the hospital, kept him informed of events in Brownsville and at the hospital.[84] She was still living in Memphis, where she taught school for more than 25 years, first at Whitehaven High and, from 1948 until her retirement in 1967, at East High. At East, which opened the year she came, Elizabeth had many roles, including those of faculty adviser, English teacher, sponsor of the *Quill and Scroll*, and yearbook adviser. Miss Wills was

Elizabeth "Bee" Wills (1902–1995), faculty advisor, 1953 Memphis East High Yearbook, "The Mustang"

---

84   Haywood County Memorial Hospital continued to serve Haywood County until January 29, 1974, when it closed and its patients were transferred to Haywood Park General Hospital, a replacement hospital built and owned by Hospital Corporation of America. When the old building was razed, some of the brick was used on the east and north steps of the Haywood County Courthouse and several thousand bricks were saved until 1985 when they were used to build the new Haywood County Public Health Building. The bronze dedication plaque was also saved. In 2008, plans were made to mount it in the Haywood County Museum on College Hill as a reminder of the one-third of a century that Haywood County Memorial Hospital served the people of Haywood County so well. Haywood County used the money it received from Hospital Corporation of America to establish a private trust, Wills Memorial Foundation, that makes grants to young people from the county who are interested in health-related subjects in college. The trustees in 2008 were Mayor Webb Follin Banks, County Executive Franklin Smith, Pat H. Mann Jr., Cristy Smith and Sandra Silverstein. A Tennessee Historical Society marker marks the site on College Street where Haywood County Memorial hospital once stood.

revered by her students at East as being demanding but fair.

Marilyn McIntosh, who graduated from East in 1955, would never forget Miss Wills. "She was the best teacher I ever had," Marilyn told the author in 2008. "She was perky and had a precious sense of humor but put up with no monkey business." After retirement, Elizabeth continued to live in Memphis where her cousin, Bobby Mann, provided companionship and assistance and where she was an active member at Idlewild Presbyterian Church.[85] In the 1970s and early 1980s, Elizabeth lived in an apartment at 188 South McLean.

When Elizabeth moved to Park Manor Apartments in Nashville in 1985, Ridley Wills II took her a copy of *Summons to Memphis*, Peter Taylor's new novel that won a Pulitzer Prize. When Ridley asked Elizabeth if she knew Peter Taylor, she answered, "yes." Ridley then asked when she last saw him. Her response was "When Hillsman brought him in a box to our house in Brownsville to Sunday dinner." Ridley realized that would have happened 68 years earlier when Hillsman Taylor, of Trenton, Tennessee, brought his baby son, Peter, to dinner at Mann Wills' house in 1917.

With her smaller apartment, Elizabeth gave away some of her prized possessions. This may have been when Elizabeth gave papers and books that had been given her by the poet, Vachel Lindsay, to the Illinois Historical Preservation Agency for the upkeep of the Vachel Lindsay home in Springfield, Illinois, that was open to the public. The papers and books were to be kept in the house, where Lindsay was born and where he died. Elizabeth visited the museum in Springfield, where she was interviewed about her relationship with the poet in the 1920s.

Soon after moving to Nashville, Elizabeth gave Ridley Wills II a sketch of her grandfather, and his great grandfather, William Thaddeus Wills M.D. After Ridley's son, Morgan J. Wills, became a physician, Ridley gave the sketch to him. Elizabeth Wills died February 26, 1995, at age 92. She was buried in Oakwood Cemetery in Brownsville, near the graves of so many of her relatives. The Rev. Joseph R. Thornton III, a cousin, performed the graveside ceremony. Afterward, Pat M. Mann

---

85   Elizabeth Wills was president of the Business Women's Circles at Idlewild Presbyterian Church for two years. On the Tri Delta Sorority's 73rd anniversary banquet at the Colonial Country Club in Memphis, she was named Tri Delta's "Woman of the Year." She was also a past president of the Tennessee Education Association, Western Section.

Jr., another cousin, hosted a gathering for the family, many of whom had not been to Brownsville for years. Soon after Miss Wills' death, her nephew, Wills Oglesby, gave more of her papers and books relating to Vachel Lindsay to the Illinois Historical Preservation Agency for inclusion in the collection at Lindsay's home.

Jesse Wills, his sister, Mamie Craig, and their mother, Mrs. Jessie Wills, never forgot that before Ridley Wills' mental breakdown in 1936, he had intended to endow a psychiatric treatment center at Vanderbilt University Hospital. Jesse, Mamie Craig and Mrs. Wills decided in 1957 to make that center a reality. They each made substantial gifts of National Life stock to the university for the establishment of the W.R. Wills Center for Psychiatric Treatment and Research. At the dedication on January 6, 1961, Chancellor Harvey Branscomb termed the gifts, "A contribution to this medical school and to this community of first importance." The ceremony, in the amphitheater of the Vanderbilt Medical School, was attended by members of the Wills family and the Vanderbilt Board of Trust, as well as a number of professional workers in the field of psychiatry. Special guests were Mrs. W.R. Wills, widow of the former National Life and Accident Insurance Company president for whom the center was named, and his son, Jesse E. Wills, a member of the Vanderbilt Board of Trust. The Wills Center, which would occupy the fourth floor of the south wing of the hospital, was designed to accommodate 17 children in large, dormitory-style rooms. A large play area was provided on the same floor. In addition to the Wills' substantial gift, the $700,000 Wills Center was financed from university funds, a grant from the Ford Foundation and other government funds. Dr. Douglas Powers, chief of the children's psychiatric unit, said "This is the only unit of its kind in the state able to offer diagnosis and treatment to a limited number of children all over the state, and afford a setting for training and research."

An editorial in the *Nashville Banner* said, "Philanthropy marked the long lifetime of the man, the late W.R. Wills, whose name it wears, and in whose memory his family gave a substantial gift for construction of the center…Not only Vanderbilt, but the community and the region are indebted to the Wills family for the generous gift – a spirit of giving in keeping with the memory they honor."[86] The plaque, designed by Robert "Bob" McGaw, is still displayed in the hospital, although the center no longer exists. The text reads as follows:

Dedicated to the Memory of
WILLIAM RIDLEY WILLS
A member of the Board of Trust of Vanderbilt University

THE
W. R. WILLS CENTER

For
Psychiatric
Treatment and Research

Presented by his wife and children
1959

When Mother Wills' oldest grandson, Matt Wills, married Julia Harrison "Judy" Ryan, of Charlottesville, Virginia, in June 1958, she made the trip to Virginia for the wedding. This was Mrs. Wills' first trip to Charlottesville and the first time she had experienced the beauty of the Blue Ridge Mountains. Mother Wills loved staying at the Farmington Country Club and was immediately taken with Judy and her parents, Commander and Mrs. Phillip Ryan. It was a memorable weekend for an 85-year-old, and one she enjoyed talking about when she returned to Nashville.

In 1960, Mamie Craig and Senter Crook bought a handsome home at 580 Jackson Blvd., which had been nearly completed as a speculation house by a Nashville contractor, Omar Jordan. Senter kept tabs on the house's final construction work, making sure that Mr. Jordan personalized it to fit the Crooks' tastes and needs. Mamie Craig, who suffered from anxiety and depression, just as her father and her Uncle Mann had, was not available to help with the decisions facing Senter. She was a patient

---

86   *Nashville Banner*, January 6-7, 1961.

at Highland Hospital in Asheville, North Carolina. Originally known as Dr. Robert S. Carroll's Sanitarium, the hospital provided a program of treatment for mental and nervous disorders and addictions, and had been operated by the Neuropsychiatric Department of Duke University since 1948. Mamie Craig went there even though a tragic fire in 1948 had destroyed the main building and taken the lives of nine women, including Zelda Fitzgerald, the wife of F. Scott Fitzgerald.

With their new one-story house on one of the larger lots in Belle Meade, the Crooks sold their home on Sheppard Place. By then, all of Mamie Craig's children were grown. Two of them, Eleanor and Phoebe, were married, the latter marrying Marvin J. Nischan on December 19, 1958. George was the only child to live there with his mother and stepfather.

As Eleanor was the oldest of the six Wills grandchildren, her four oldest children were the oldest in their generation on Eleanor's side of the family. Five of Eleanor and Everett's children – Eleanor Craig Kelley (1953), Josephine Wills Kelley (1955), Phoebe Wade Kelley (1957), Alton Wade Kelley (1959) and Jessie Palmer Kelley (1962) – were born before their great-grandmother Wills died. Only Edward Everett Kelley (1966) was born after her death. The oldest three have clear memories of Mamma Wills.

Craig recalled in 2008, "We would visit with Mamma Wills in her study, and play with wooden blocks on the floor. Jo and I painfully remember she would affectionately pinch us with her bright lacquered fingernails, which would always leave us with marks. To this day when we see red lacquered fingernails, we laugh about how it looks like Mamma Wills." Craig remembered that her great grandmother had a myna bird in a big cage "like the one at Chester's Department Store," and that Mamma Wills enjoyed taking her and Jo to get spring coats and hats from Albert Merville at Loveman's. Craig later concluded that Mamma Wills was fond of hats since her father ran a hat store. As small children, Craig and Jo would sometimes eat lunch with Mamma Wills. They were always formal affairs in the dining room and did not start until Lem rang the gong at 1 p.m. to announce that lunch was served. Willie Mae, the cook, often made popovers using a cast iron popover pan.

Craig and Josephine's memories of their grandmother, Maymay, are even stronger. When Craig was three or four, she remembers being taken to Douglas, Michigan, where her grandparents had a big, frame house on Lake Michigan. Craig particularly loved playing in the wet sand on the beach. In later years, Mamie Craig and Senter had a vacation home at Bluegrass Country Club on Old Hickory Lake. Craig Adkisson recalled in 2008 that "Senter would buy a new one [boat] every time Uncle George would sink one. Several of us would get to go with them and spend the night there overnight, which we loved. We would ride in the boat, then sit out on the lawn in aluminum lawn chairs and look at the lake. Sometimes, we would even stay two nights. Maymay had wooden bunk beds for Jo and I, which we loved."

Phoebe and Marvin's oldest child, Mamie Craig "Mimi" Nischan, was born in 1960. When she was small, her mother would put her in her best dress every Sunday morning and take her to have breakfast with her great grandmother Wills at her house on Belle Meade Boulevard. Then

Pictured from left to right: Miss Millie Williams, Margaret (Mrs. Frederick W.) Williams, Miss Margaret Williams, Jessie (Mrs. Ridley) Wills, Jesse Wills and Ellen Buckner (Mrs. Jesse) Wills ar the wedding of Ellen McClung Wills and Lt. Williams Swift Martin III, U.S.A., West Point, New York, June 8, 1960.

Phoebe and Marvin would take Mimi to church.

When Jessie's granddaughter, Ellen McClung Wills, became engaged to Williams Swift Martin III, a cadet at West Point, her parents gave an engagement party at the Belle Meade Mansion on Monday evening, December 28, 1959. Joining Mr. and Mrs. Wills in welcoming guests were Swift's parents, Mr. and Mrs. Williams Swift Martin Jr., of Washington, D.C.; Ellen's aunt and uncle, Mamie Craig and Senter Crook; her aunt, Mrs. Mary Harding Ragland, of Richmond, Va.; and Ellen's grandmother, Mrs. Ridley Wills. Mamma Wills had a good time at the engagement party and remembered how much she enjoyed going to Matt and Judy's wedding 18 months earlier, Consequently, she decided to go to the wedding that was to be held in the West Point Post Chapel on graduation day, June 8, 1960. When Swift's grandmother, Minnie English Stone (Mrs. W.S.) Martin, heard that Mrs. Wills was coming, she decided she would also attend. After all, she was only 82, while Mrs. Wills was 87. Mamma Wills' roommate on the trip was her husband's niece, Mrs. Trousdale Sturdivant, whom she loved but with whom she also fussed. At the beginning of the wedding, just before Mendelsson's wedding march began, Catherine, the African-American maid of Gen. and Mrs. George A. Lincoln,[87] asked Ellen how she could help. Ellen suggested she arrange her wedding gown train. As the organist played the wedding march, the Nashville contingent was aghast when they realized that Catherine, with train in hand, had followed Ellen and her father down the aisle. Those guests not from Nashville took this in stride, assuming that this was an old Southern custom. Mamma Wills and Mrs. W.S. Martin got along fine, posing for a picture. When Mamma Wills later saw the picture, her comment was, "Don't we look pretty?" The trip to Ellen's wedding must have been one of the last trips Mamma Wills made.

In her last years, Mamma Wills was concerned that her son, Jesse, was working too hard at National Life and might either die prematurely or suffer a breakdown similar to the one that his father had experienced. A manifestation of her concern was revealed when she wrote her

---

87   The Lincolns had befriended Ellen for four years, having enjoyed having her stay on the third floor of their home at West Point whenever she came to see Swift.

grandson, Matt Wills, then living in Colorado Springs, a brief letter in which she told Matt that she might need him to come to her aid sometime. Only later did Matt interpret the letter to mean that, in the event something catastrophic happened to her son, she thought he, as the oldest grandson, should move back to Tennessee.

Jessie Ely Wills executed a codicil to her last will and testament on October 12, 1964, four months before her death. In the codicil, she made various bequests, using National Life stock to make them. The stock gifts and beneficiaries were:

Two thousand shares to The Downtown Presbyterian Church, three hundred shares to the Haywood County Memorial Hospital, one hundred shares to each of the following people: Mrs. Mary Nelson Ream, of Atlanta; Margaret Nelson (Mrs. William. Frederick Jr.) Williams, of Providence, Rhode Island; Mrs. Mary Hager Englesing, of Saint Louis, Mo.; Mrs. Margaret Hager, of St. Louis; Miss Elizabeth Wills, of Memphis; and Mrs. Trousdale Wills Sturdivant, of Nashville; and 50 shares to each of the following: Herbert Wills Oglesby, son of Harriette Wills Oglesby, deceased; and Mann Wills Oglesby, of Nashville, son of Harriette Wills Oglesby, deceased. Mrs. Wills also left cash bequests to four servants: Lemie Roosevelt Wilson $400, Lura Browder Burrus $300, Willie Mae Ballentine $150, and Nannie Moore Brown $150.

In the same codicil, Mrs. Wills modified her will as follows: "During the lifetime of my son, Jesse Wills, instead of paying the entire income from his trust to him, the trustee shall pay him one-fourth of his said share of income and shall divide the remaining three-fourths of his said share of income equally among his children, Matt, Ridley and Ellen Wills." She also changed the trustee from First American National Bank to Third National Bank.

At her death on February 18, 1965, Mrs. Wills' will created a trust for the benefit of her daughter, Mamie Craig Crook, during her lifetime and, following her death, would pay income to her lineal descendants. Third National Bank was trustee for this trust that would terminate on the death of the last of the following persons to die: Mamie Craig

Crook, Eleanor Clark Kelley, Phoebe Clark Nischan and George Wills Crook.

Used to being independent, it was difficult for Mrs. Wills, in her late 80s and early 90s, to have a sitter or practical nurse living with her at her home on Belle Meade Boulevard. Frustrated at her inability to be self-reliant, she was not easy to work for. One winter day, Mrs. Wills went out on her back porch to feed the birds only to slip on the ice and fall. Unable to get up or call loudly enough to attract attention to her plight, she lay there for some time. As a result, she developed pneumonia, causing her physician to recommend that she be taken to Vanderbilt Hospital.[88] Although she did not want to do so, she entered Vanderbilt where, after a short illness, she died at age 92 on February 18, 1965. Fortunately, Mrs. Wills' final illness was brief, and she retained her mental facilities until the end. The *Nashville Banner* reported her death that evening. The article said that she was educated at Ward's Seminary and had married Ridley Wills in 1898. It also listed her cultural interests, reporting that she was a charter member of both Cheekwood and The Downtown Presbyterian Church, and that, having a lifelong interest in gardening and civic affairs, she was a member of the Colonial Dames of America, the Belle Meade Country Club, the Garden Study Club of Nashville, and the Centennial Club. The write-up mentioned her husband's and son's involvement in National Life & Accident Insurance Company and listed her descendants that included, in addition to her children, Jesse E. Wills and Mamie Craig Crook, six grandchildren – Eleanor (Mrs. Everett E.) Kelley; Phoebe (Mrs. Marvin J.) Nischan; George W. Crook; William Ridley Wills II, all of Nashville; Matthew B. Wills, of Colorado Springs; and Ellen (Mrs. Williams Swift) Martin, of Fort Campbell, Kentucky; and 14 great grandchildren. The next morning, *The Nashville Tennessean* reported on Mrs. Ridley Wills' death. It said that Rev. William D. Gray, Minister of The Downtown Presbyterian Church, would conduct the funeral service on Saturday, February 20, 1965. Active pallbearers were Matt B. Wills, Ridley Wills II, George W. Crook, Everett E. Kelley, Marvin J. Nischan, Capt. Williams S. Martin, C. Runcie Clements Jr., C.A. Craig

---

88   Mrs. Wills had earlier survived a bout of pneumonia that put her in Vanderbilt Hospital.

II, G. Henry Tyne, Dr. Garth E. Fort and Craig Parrish. The last five pallbearers represented the other four founding families of National Life and Accident Insurance Company. The honorary pallbearers were the directors of National Life.

The *Nashville Banner* published an editorial in memory of Mrs. Wills in which the newspaper identified her areas of service as "motherhood and home-making, her church, her charities, and her ties to the cultural in the realm of mind and spirit. She loved her beautiful and planted flowers, and her community. Hers was a hospitable home and hers the response of heart-felt interest in every civic duty. In philanthropy, she shared a family characteristic of generosity. In 1959, she and her children established the W.R. Wills Center for Psychiatric Treatment and Research at Vanderbilt University." The concluding sentence said, "In every heart that knew her, the memory of Mrs. William Ridley Wills will be an enduring monument."

Craig, Josephine and Phoebe Kelley went with their parents to Mamma Wills' home during the visitation period before her funeral. Elizabeth Wills, who had come up from Memphis, asked the girls, then twelve, nine and seven, "Have you seen Mamma Wills yet?" The girls were silent and confused. Each thought she had died. Elizabeth continued, "She's up in her room. Go see her." So, the girls excitedly ran upstairs and went in Mamma Wills' bedroom. There, they saw Mamma Wills' body in her own bed with the sheet pulled up. Obviously, she was dead. They instantly turned on their heels and ran out. Ellen Wills Martin remembered that, when she saw her grandmother lying in state in her bedroom, Mrs. Wills' hair had been dyed red, the color it had been when she was much younger. Ellen's impression was that this pleased her father, Jesse.

Upon the death of Jessie Ely Wills, trust B for her benefit thereupon terminated and the principal thereof was duly distributed to trusts C and D in accordance with the said Indenture dated October 23, 1930.

Not long after his mother's death, Jesse Wills and Bob Sturdivant opened her lock box at First American National Bank. There Jesse found a letter his mother had written him a few days after publishing her last will and testament 1n 1950. She said, "My life since dad's going would have been so lonely had it not been for you and your children." She also wrote, "We have had our misunderstandings but I hope you will not remember them and think of me with as much affection as you think I deserve." She added, "I pray not be a burden or helpless." Mrs. Wills explained why she left certain things to certain children or grandchildren, and also wrote, "If Ellen and sister don't care for them [a gold chain and plain gold bracelet] give them to Trousdale who for some reason has always seemed to love me. You all will no doubt wonder too."

This letter indicates that Mrs. Wills and Jesse were not always close. Nevertheless, they loved each other and she knew, long before her death, how successful and respected he had become in the community. In 1958, he had been elected to the Vanderbilt Board of Trust, just as his father had been in 1934. On January 1, 1963, he became president and CEO of the National Life and Accident Insurance Company, then the largest life insurance company in the South. This happened exactly 32 years after his father became president of National Life.

Senter Crook, who had a history of heart problems, including a heart attack in 1955, died of a heart attack on August 31, 1965. He and Mamie Craig's marriage had lasted 19 years and had worked well for both. Mamie Craig had needed a husband, and Senter had needed a family.

It took Jesse Wills more than four years to settle his mother's estate with the IRS. In May 1969, he and the IRS agreed that her taxable estate was $4,508,490.22. The total death taxes amounted to $2,013,051.91 plus debts of $6,848.24 and funeral and administrative expenses of $107,715.60

Not long after being named president of National Life in 1963, Jesse Wills wrote Harry Randall, a close iris-breeding friend who lived in England. Jesse said: "I have taken on a heavy and increased responsibility which is going to be particularly onerous the first year because of a great amount of travel that will be involved. I have known for some time that this was coming, and felt it was a duty I could not avoid. My father had a great deal to do with the founding of this company and was vice president for many years and then president for a few years until his illness terminated this in 1936. My tenure of office may be relatively brief. The normal retirement date for me would be August 1964, but active service may be extended for a year at a time until August 31, 1969.

My recent predecessors have all used this extension, and, if my health holds up, I will probably do the same thing for part of the time, at least, though at sometime during that period I may move up to the chairman of the board."

Jesse's prediction came true. After serving as president for two years, he was succeeded by G. Daniel Brooks in 1965, and became chairman of the board of directors. On August 31, 1967, after 45 years of service, Jesse Wills retired from National Life. He was 68 years old. Thirteen years later, Alan Costa, who was writing his Ph.D. dissertation at Vanderbilt on Jesse Wills at the time, interviewed Brooks. He asked Brooks if Jesse had been a figurehead at National Life. Brooks said "no." He told Costa that Jesse did a wonderful job even though he thought Jesse would have been happier had he been a college professor. Brooks then said, "Jesse epitomized everything that was good in the company and followed the best principles of honor and integrity which were the basic foundation of the company. He was a symbol of everything that was good and fine about the company. Jesse was not a frontrunner. He didn't push himself but he got a lot done."[89]

With his children grown, Jesse Wills began writing poetry again in the late 1950s, producing *Early and Late* in 1959. In September of that year, Juris Pivics, secretary to Professor Hohenberg, Columbia University, a member the advisory board of Pulitzer Prizes, wrote Vanderbilt expressing interest in their recent publication of *Early and Late*. Pivics said, "I sincerely hope that you will enter it or at least consider its nomination in the near future." The book was nominated for a Pulitzer Prize in poetry but did not win. The ever-modest Jesse never talked about the prestigious nomination. Allen Tate reviewed *Early and Late* and wrote, "The mind at work in these poems is as modern and far-reaching as any in our time."

Jesse followed up with *Conversation Piece and Other Poems* in 1965, *Nashville and Other Poems* in 1973, and *Selected Poems* in 1975. Because of his lifelong interest in American Indians, he wrote a book, *Meditations*

---

89   Alan M. Costa, *The Biography of a Fugitive: An Evaluation of the life and Work of Jesse E. Wills*, Dissertation submitted to the Faculty of the Graduate School of Vanderbilt University in partial fulfillment of the requirements for the degree of Doctor of Philosophy in English, December 1980, p. 22.

on the American Indian, that was published in 1971. Finally, he published *A Diversity of Interests* in 1976, only a year before he died. This book includes six essays that Jesse wrote in a 15-year period between 1961 and 1975. They "represent the author's avocations, including horticulture, archaeology, ornithology, poetry, and a nostalgic esteem for bygone trains and ships, Christmases, circuses and certain books."[90]

The *Vanderbilt Hustler* announced, on August 31, 1973, "The most extensive collection of Fugitive and Agrarian materials to date is being compiled now at the Joint University Library. It will be known as the Jesse E. Wills Collection, honoring the last Fugitive poet to remain in Nashville, now 73 years old, a lifetime board of trust member and the man Allen Tate once described as 'the most natural and powerful talent among the Fugitives.'"

Jessie and Ridley Wills' daughter, Mamie Craig Crook, died at age 74 on May 25, 1976. Her funeral was at Harpeth Presbyterian Church, and burial was at the Crook lot in Mt. Olivet Cemetery. Born in Bristol on June 11, 1901, during a brief period when her father was working for the Virginia Coal, Iron and Coke Company there, Mrs. Crook grew up in Nashville on Patterson Street and Louise Avenue. Educated in Nashville and at Holton Arms School in Washington, D.C., she was a founding member of the Junior League of Nashville, the Centennial Club and the Garden Club of Nashville. Mamie Craig was survived by two daughters, Eleanor (Mrs. Everett E.) Kelley and Phoebe (Mrs. Marvin J.) Nischan, a son, George Wills Crook; a brother, Jesse Ely Wills, and 10 grandchildren. She would have been pleased that George would go on to live in her home on Jackson Boulevard with his wife, Emily Keeble "Em" Crook, and their children, George Wills Crook Jr. and Catherine Crook.

Jesse Wills outlived Mamie Craig by 10 months. When he died March 4, 1977, of pulmonary insufficiency due to pulmonary fibrosis, the community of Nashville lost a multitalented man who returned many times over the talents that were God-given to him. Tributes came from many organizations, including resolutions of appreciation from the boards of Vanderbilt University, Montgomery Bell Academy, The

---

90   FOREWARD, *Diversity of Interests.*

Downtown Presbyterian Church and the Nashville City Bank and Trust Company. Rob Roy Purdy, vice-chancellor of Vanderbilt University, spoke at a memorial service for Wills at The Downtown Presbyterian Church. Following are some of the words Purdy used to eulogize his longtime friend:

Jesse's creative talent began to blossom at Vanderbilt, where as a member of the Fugitives, the esteem of his fellow poets is on record by testimonials such as 'his was the most natural and powerful talent of the Fugitives.

Jesse's modesty and his ever-reaching desire to search for things untried were to deter him from becoming a professional man of letters. His poetic voice was muted during his middle years, which he spent trying out his Midas touch in fields of infinite variety.

Success was golden in whatever he reached for. He gave devoted attention to his family and his business, and still found time to lend his talents to the study of iris-growing, birds, archaeology, the American Indian, World War II, and matters of religion. His Supremacy in all he tried was that of a latter-day Renaissance man. No other Nashvillian and few persons anywhere have excelled in diverse ways comparable to this.

For those of us whose fortune is to receive this legacy, his verses make immortal his wide-ranging intellect, his sense of beauty, his gentleness of spirit. This spirit, guided by an indomitable will, shone through all his living and all his dying – even through his last travail, when he met with calmness and fortitude the infirmities of the flesh.

When Jesse Wills died, friends were concerned about his widow, Ellen Buckner Wills, whose charm, graciousness and warmth had long endeared her to all her friends, to so many National Life field employees and their wives, whom she met at company leaders' meetings, and to many friends of her children. Ellen coped surprisingly well without her beloved husband and lived to see her 92nd birthday. For most of the years after Jesse's death, she continued to live at Meade Haven. When a fire caused extensive smoke damage to the house in 1994, she moved to St. Paul Retirement Center where she made many new friends and so enjoyed their company. Despite the increasing infirmities of old age,

Ellen rejoiced to see her grandson, Ridley Wills III, restore and move with his wife, Betsy, and their daughter, Meade, to Meade Haven in the summer of 1995, shortly before the birth of their son, Ridley Wills IV.[91] Ellen also attended the official opening of the Wills Visitor Center at Belle Meade Plantation on October 26, 1998. It was dedicated in honor of her and her son and daughter-in-law, Ridley and Irene Wills. Ellen Buckner Wills died at St. Paul Retirement Center September 18, 2000.

Jessie and Ridley Wills were proud of their son and daughter, Jesse and Mamie Craig, and of their grandchildren: Eleanor, Matt, Phoebe, Ridley, Ellen and George. The Wills would have also been proud of their great grandchildren. Hopefully, by reading this book, these descendants and their children will gain a fuller appreciation for how much Jessie Ely and Ridley Wills accomplished during the time God gave them on this earth, how well they lived their lives and how bountifully they provided for their descendants.

---

91   When Ridley Wills IV was small, he told people, who asked his name, "My name is Ridley Wills. There are four of us but one of us is dead," meaning his great great grandfather, William Ridley Wills.

INDEX

Hutchison, Robert H., 35-38
Jackson, Erwin, 157
Jackson, Henriette Weaver (Mrs. Granbery, Jr.), 70
Jackson, Miss Katherine, 157
Jackson, Miss Susan, 157
Jackson, Robert, 157
Jackson, Robert Fenner, 110
Jackson, Trousdale Sturdivant (Mrs. Erwin S.), 157
Jamison, David Shelby, 24
Jamison, Eleanor Shelby, 24
Jamison, Miss Charlotte, 18, 24, 25
Jamison, William Caldwell, 24, 25
Johnson, Stanley, 65
Johnston, Albert Sidney, 19
Jonas, Leopold, 44
Jones, Andrew Roy, M.D., 153
Jones, Edgar, 39
Jones, Jane Millard Oglesby, M.D., 153
Jones, Miss Judith, 9
Jones, Miss Ridley, 8-9
Jones, Thomas E., 103, 104
Jones, W. D., 138
Jordan, Omar, 162
Julian, W. H., 46
Keeton, R. T., M.D., 84
Kelley, Alton Wade, 163
Kelley, Edward Everett, 163
Kelley, Eleanor Clark (Mrs. Everett), 137, 167, 173
Kelley, Everett Edward, 112, 163, 167
Kelley, Jimmy, 91

Kelley, Miss Eleanor Craig, 163, 164, 168
Kelley, Miss Jessie Palmer, 163
Kelley, Miss Josephine Wills "Jo," 163, 168
Kelley, Miss Phoebe Wade, 163, 168
Kellond, F. E., 123
Kirby, Edwin M. "Ed," 101
Kirkland, James H., 65, 99, 126
Kirkland, Mary Henderson (Mrs. James H.), 126
Kirkman, Van Leer, 77
Kirkpatrick, Hugh F., 51
Kirkpatrick, Mary G. (Mrs. Hugh F.), 51, 70
Kirkpatrick, Miss Emma, 45
Kleeman, Edward, 38
Knox, Lois (Mrs. John), 104
Knox, Mrs. J. Hugh, 132
Knox, Rev. John, 104
Landon, Alfred, 103
Lavender, Mrs., 112
Lawless, J. W., 42
Lawrence, Miss Ann, 17
Lawson, Mrs. Charlotte, 87
Leake, James O., 46
Leake, Mrs. James O., 46
Leathers, Walter S., M.D., 117
Lee, Luke, 55
Lee, Mr., 96
Lee, Mrs., 96
Lee, Robert E., 19
LeSueur, Thomas R., 118, 119
Lewis, Miss Gertrude, 90

Thornton, Macon, 47, 74, 100, 108, 120, 123

Thornton, Marion, 74

Thornton, Mildred (Mrs. John C.), 84

Thornton, Miss Ruth, 74

Thornton, Nicholas Perkins, 74

Thornton, Nicholas Perkins, Jr., 74

Thornton, Rev. Joseph Richard III, 160

Thornton, Robert, 74

Tigrett, Isaac B., 136

Tipton, James, 86

Tirrill, Willard O., 101

Trabue, Charles C., 109, 128

Trabue, Charles C., Jr.

Trabue, William D. "Will," 120

Tucker, Miss Dot, 51

Tucker, R. O., M.D. 105

Turrentine, Mrs. Dee Waller, 106

Tyne, George Henry, 90, 151, 168

Tyne, Jane Ratterman (Mrs. Thomas J.), 78, 92, 106, 124

Tyne, Thomas J., 39–42, 59, 60, 78, 92, 106, 123, 124, 127

Uncle Alfred, 6, 85

Vance, Rev. James I., 33, 89, 101, 111, 125

Wade, Gideon, 77

Walker, Miss Mattie, 13

Wallace, Clarence B., 56, 67, 125

Waller, James, 90

Warner, Edwin, 20

Warner, Joseph H., 20

Warner, Percy, 20, 77

Warner, Susan R. (Mrs. Edwin), 143

Warren, Robert Penn, 64

Watkins, Sam, 19

Weatherford, Willis D., 103

Weaver, Robert "Spud," 106, 109

Webb, Edward I., Jr., 57

Webb, William R. "Sawnie," 3

Weber, Beulah (Mrs. H. C.), 77

Weber, H. C., 77

Webster, Daniel, 29

Wentzel, William, 107

West, Olin, M.D., 52

West, Olin, Jr., 52

West, Robert, 52

West, Susie Hunter (Mrs. Olin), 52

White, David Walker, 120

White, James, 26

White, Newton, 38-40

Whitehurst, Fred, M.D., 84

Whiteside, Agnes (Mrs. Henry C.), 73

Whiteside, David, 28

Whiteside, Henry C., 29, 73

Whiteside, Jenkin, 28

Whiteside, Margaret Ann Robinson (Mrs. Thomas Cooper), 22–25, 29, 135

Whiteside, Miss Ada, 15

Whiteside, Miss Margaret "Maggie," 15, 29, 30

Whiteside, Miss Mary E., 26, 29

Whiteside, Miss Ruth, 18, 25, 26, 29

Whiteside, Mrs. Henry C., 33

Life 37-39; elected secretary and treasurer of National Life, 40; return to Nashville, 42; purchases home on Broad Street, 42; purchases farms, 45, 116, 129, 138; interest in children, 48, 70; purchases home on Patterson Street, 77; athletic interests, 49, 68, 107, 108; builds home on Louise Avenue, 51; elected Deacon, 51; fishing trips, 49, 94, 105; vacations 54, 98, 105, 111, 112, 124; dedication of new home office, 60; WSM founded, 60; illnesses, 60, 67, 74, 124, 126, 127, 128, 138, 151; elected ruling elder 66; Mamie Craig's marriage, 72, 73; National Life's first public stock offering, 76; Purchases land for new home on Curtiswood Lane, 77; gift of Haywood County Hospital, 83–86; Jesse's marriage, 88, 89; other charitable interests, 76, 101, 107, 108, 109, 132; elected president of National Life, 90; National Life celebrations, 92, 123; New Deal attitudes, 102, 103; community service, 103, 104, 110, 117, 125; WSM Radio talks, 109, 112, 128; election to Vanderbilt Board of Trust, 110; church experiences, 111, 125; named vice-chairman

of National Life, 130; death of, 150; W. R. Wills Psychiatric Center established, 161

Wills, William Ridley II (son of Asa Mann Wills), 7, 32,37, 53, 54-56, 63–66, 94–100, 127 150, 156

Wills, William Ridley II (son of Jesse E. Wills), 53, 63, 75, 77, 80, 111, 112, 114, 124, 128–131, 135, 139, 154, 158, 160, 166, 167, 173

Wills, William Ridley "Bill" Wills III (grandson of Asa Mann Wills), 95–97, 136

Wills, William Ridley III (grandson of Jesse E. Wills), 173

Wills, William Ridley IV (great grandson of Jesse E. Wills), 173

Wills, William Thaddeus, M.D., 1–6, 8–10, 12, 22, 45, 83, 85, 101, 160

Wilson, Lemmie Roosevelt "Lem," 135, 137, 138, 140, 148, 163, 166

Wilson, Miss Luella Whitehead, 95

Wilson, Miss Mary, 26

Wilson, Mr., 7

Wimbish, Shack, 48

Wisdom, Mrs. Mae Cox, 153

Witherspoon, Rev. Jere, D.D., 24

Wofford, Charles P., 39, 44, 46

Printed in the United States
132552LV00002B/6/P

9 787770 435508